MW01491090

GALLOPING OFF IN ALL DIRECTIONS

An Anthology for Horse Lovers

St. Martin's Press/New York

First published by Angus and Robertson (UK) Ltd, 16 Ship Street, Brighton, Sussex in 1978
Copyright © Angus and Robertson · Publishers 1978

This edition published in the United States of America by
St Martin's Press, 175 Fifth Avenue, New York, N.Y. 10010

Extract from *Stunt* by John Baxter © John Baxter
Extract from *Let Sleeping Vets Lie* © James Herriot
Extract from *Papa Hemingway* by A. E. Hotchner © 1955, 1959, 1966 A. E. Hotchner
White Hunter, Red Fox by Art Buchwald © Art Buchwald
The Hairy Joys of Hangin' On by Dotson Rader © Dotson Rader

The Publishers gratefully acknowledge the following for permission to reprint extracts from published works: Mr Art Buchwald for permission to reprint the article entitled *White Hunter, Red Fox*. A. D. Peters & Co Ltd for permission to reprint an extract from *Stunt* by John Baxter, St Martin's Press for permission to reprint an extract from *Let Sleeping Vets Lie* by James Herriot, Mr A. E. Hotchner for permission to reprint an extract from *Papa Hemingway* by A. E. Hotchner, International Creative Management for permission to reprint *The Hairy Joys of Hangin' On* by Dotson Rader. Cartoons by Norman Thelwell from Angels on Horseback Copyright © 1957, 1958 by E. P. Dutton & Co, and reprinted with their permission; and from Thelwell's Riding Academy, Copyright © 1963, 1964 by Norman Thelwell and Beaverbrook Newspapers Ltd, reprinted by permission of the publishers, E. P. Dutton.

For use of the illustrations:
The Association of Professional Cowboys p. 174.   Australian War Memorial pp. 117, 122, 124, 126, 128.   Lord Patrick Beresford pp. 83, 91.   Cinema International Corporation p. 168.   Gerry Cranham, p. 112.   Bob Dear pp. 95, 150, 165.   Srdja Djukanovic pp. 84, 135, 136, 138.   Eyre Methuen pp. 178, 179, 181.   Clive Hiles p. 80.   International Racing Bureau p. 107.   Dr Hans Jesse p. 98.   Michael Joseph Ltd p. 51.   Richard Meade p. 79.   M.G.M. Pictures Ltd pp. 3, 6.   News Ltd pp. 21, 28.   Planned Public Relations International p. 111.   Mike Roberts p. 86.   Rogers and Cowan p. 172.   Sport and General pp. 153, 156, 163, 169.   Swiss National Tourist Office pp. 41, 45, 46.   Stella A. Walker p. 100.   Sunday Times p. 147.   Warner Bros p. 1.   Derek Ware p. 4.   Western Americana Picture Library pp. 11, 13, 63.   Thomas A. Wilkie p. 185.   The United States Travel Service pp. 16, 17.
The drawings on pp. 52, 54, 58 and 60 are by Derek Alder

All rights reserved. For information, write:
St. Martin's Press, Inc., 175 Fifth Ave., New York, N.Y. 10010
Printed in Great Britain
Library of Congress Catalog Card Number: 78-52331
First published in the United States of America in 1978

ISBN 0 312 31576 7

H B M Typesetting, Chorley, Lancashire

Printed in Great Britain by Ebenezer Baylis & Son Ltd.
The Trinity Press, Worcester, and London

CONTENTS

1 THEY SHOOT HORSES DON'T THEY?
Horses as stars and victims in Hollywood

John Baxter

The word 'Hollywood' has long meant two things: a large hunk of real estate in Los Angeles and a synonym for the American motion picture industry. Whichever meaning you choose, you can truthfully say the horse was a real pioneer of Hollywood, and one of its most consistently resolute and worthwhile denizens. Since movies began, one good trained horse has been worth fifty actors, a thousand agents and any number you care to name of studio producers. These are conservative figures.

First, consider Hollywood as soil, trees and general landscape. Here the horse has superb credentials as a pioneer. In its first transformation from wasteland, 'Hollywood' was a genuine ranch, so named by the wife of Horace Henderson Wilcox for the 120 unappealing acres he bought in 1894. So pastoral Hollywood had its equine residents long before the invasions of hand-cranked cameras, Jewish-moguls-in-embryo, megaphones, tyrants in leather leggings, Chaplin's cane and moustache, Pickford's curls, careening jalopies and the first of countless corn-fed naiads with astonishing superstructures.

By 1910 the flickering Western was a staple of the fledgling movie business; foundation layers of legend had begun to obliterate the reality. Bronco Billy Anderson had already ground out 376 one-reel Westerns in Montana, Colorado and California. A few years later Cecil B. DeMille made the first of three versions of The Squaw Man; *the smell of oats, saddle leather, horses' and extras' sweat and crushed sagebrush was strong in the clear Hollywood air.*

From the outset horses were in big demand. For Westerns alone, studios needed to put them underneath and in front of all kinds of people: cowboys, Indians, cavalry troopers, homesteaders, bandits, bushwhackers, marshals and sheriffs, Pony Express riders, gunslingers, rustlers, posses, vigilantes, scouts, bounty hunters, range bosses, wagon masters, gingham-clad schoolmarms, silent strangers from nowhere, Civil War soldiers. And . . . the unlikeliest heroes ever to gallop to the rescue in the final reel: the Ku Klux Klansmen in Griffith's The Birth of a Nation. *There was a call, too, for horses in a host of other productions – chariot teams in Biblical epics, mounts for Crusaders, jousting knights, musketeers,*

Yak Canutt's Running W harness puts down an outlaw in the opening sequence of *The Wild Bunch*. The released hook can be seen beneath the horse.

I

Bengal Lancers, Afghan tribesmen, Attila the Hun's hordes, lusty Arab sheikhs, racetrack jockeys and so on.

These horses had to be taught special skills: how to stand still in a melée; how to ignore gunshots, explosions, flaming buildings, collapsing bridges; how to survive leaps over chasms and galloping falls as dozens of Redskins and guys in black hats bit the dust. So an ancillary industry sprang up, its training ranches scattered in valleys, canyons and open country hard by the churning film capital. The men who trained and handled these horses were often the genuine article – trail-weathered cowhands from the Texas Panhandle, much-fractured veterans of travelling rodeos and wild west shows. They worked with and for those of their old range and rodeo buddies who had become stuntmen or even stars like Tom Mix, Buck Jones and Will Rogers. Many a routine film justified itself only in the climactic scene, a mounted chase with the pursued perilously dodging bullets, arrows, tomahawks, avalanches and falling boulders.

In this article, a series of extracts from his book Stunt, *John Baxter shows how important the horse has been in motion picture history. He also reveals how callous and brutally indifferent too many film makers have been to their four-footed slaves. Mr Baxter begins by talking to Yakima Canutt, the most durable and renowned of film stuntmen, about stunts with horses. Several times world rodeo champion, Canutt loped casually into Hollywood in 1923, became the acknowledged ace at his trade, invented many stunt devices and graduated into a respected second unit director.*

'When I first came down there weren't too many stunt men, and they did everything the hard way; no equipment. I did all my own stunts in my pictures, and a lot of the time stunts for someone else. I could see the advantage of using your head a little bit and creating equipment to do this work. Like falling off a horse, for instance. Sometimes a man's foot would hang in the stirrup, so he'd be dragged and hurt. Well, I had special stirrups made, open L stirrups you couldn't hang in.

In those days, you did bulldogging; you take a man off a horse by grabbing him, fall between the horses, and get run over half the time. Well, I built that up to where you jump light on the horse and go on over with the man, and then I got to where I could make it in one jump. It became a much more spectacular deal, and safer, because you cleared the horses. Then wagon wrecks. They used to dig a hole to run the wheels into or build up rocks to hit and turn the wagon over. Half the time they'd miss, or get out of the scene before the wreck. So I worked out equipment where you could drive the team on the run and when they hit the spot everything would work automatic – the team break loose, the wagon cramp and roll right on the spot.'

Canutt's technique depended on a cable of measured length staked down at one end with the other attached under the wagon directly beneath its front end. Another cable ran from the horses over the wagon and was attached to the rear of the body. The wagon tongue, which ran out between

The master Canutt in his mellow years, working as an adviser for the renowned chariot sequence from *Ben-Hur* (1959).

the horses and to which they were harnessed, was cut through, then rejoined with a spring and a pelican hook, a long hook, locked with a ring, that could be tripped open with a cable. When the measured cable tied to the bottom of the wagon ran out, it automatically opened the pelican hook and released the team (whose legs were saved by a sled-runner arrangement that kept the dragging harness from tangling them up); as the team ran forward, ahead of the wagon which was now on the verge of somersaulting, the cable attached to their harness pulled the wagon body up and forward, so that it crashed spectacularly, although the cable underneath ensured that it remained exactly where the director wanted it. The system has been perfected over the years; on *In Old Chicago* (Henry King, 1938) Cliff Lyons replaced Canutt's spring tongue with a small explosive charge, and the techniques of fastening cables to the wreck for various effects has become an art in itself. But it remains very much as Canutt originally planned it.

Canutt's most controversial trick was the notorious 'Running W' system of horse falls. Like most stunt-riding techniques, it was adapted from a familiar cowboy method. To break a horse of 'running away' each time it was released, the cowboy fixes a rope to its front legs, runs it through a ring on the saddle, ties it to his own pommel and lets the horse go. Just before it reaches the end of the rope and pitches to the ground, the breaker yells 'Whoa'; after two or three falls the call will stop it instantly. For movie stunt riders, it was invaluable.

'This gag (stunt) has caused more talk than any other,' said Canutt. 'You hear stories about horses with their legs pulled off and all this stuff. Well, this is a lot of nonsense. It's like anything else. If you do it right, it was all right. But unfortunately, somebody will always see it done a few times, then offer to do it at half price, and if he didn't know how to do it he would go out and cripple a horse. I myself, personally, rode three hundred Running Ws and never crippled a horse.

'You have a band around the horse's belly with a ring with three compartments in it. The cable is staked down, and it runs through a hole in one of the compartments, down through a hobble ring on one of the front legs, back up through another ring, down to another hobble on the other front leg, back up, and ties in the bottom compartment of the ring. The ring looks like a W – that's where it gets the name. When the cable tightens, it pulls the horse's legs up to that ring; all the strain and pull and jerk is on the saddle, it's not on the legs. The pull just snaps them up to the ring, it cuts the cable, but by that time he's got his feet up so far he can't get them back in time to save himself, so he turns a somersault. Then he gets up and away he goes.

'When I first came to Hollywood, they'd do this with a crew of men on a rope pulling at the horse's legs so he fell and floundered around. I did about two of them and I said: "Hell, there's a better way to do this than that." They were just using the old work harness cowboys used to break horses to drive, but the ring was worked from up on the side for that sort of thing and wasn't any good for picture work. So I created this ring with three compartments in it, then tested weights with a small horse and a big horse. I found that about a $\frac{1}{32}$ inch flexible aeroplane cable would break in a fall without it being noticed, leaving the horse free so he can get up again. You need a good place to do the fall, of course; soft ground for them to fall in. And the hobbles are sheepskin-lined.

'For years I kept reading these things about tying wires on horses' legs and so on, so finally I got hold of a couple of Humane Society officers and said "You people put these silly write-ups around. Why don't you come out and see how it's really done?" and they said, "Well, nobody will let us see them." I had a couple of days' work coming up and so I said, "Bring two of your men out. I'll show them every detail of it." "Fine," they said, "but remember – if you kill a horse we'll arrest you." I said, "You're perfectly welcome."

A stuntman, bringing down a horse on the bit. For a horse trained with much skill and patience, this is a gentler technique than it looks.

'Three of them came out, in fact. I showed them how we prepared the ground. Then I laced the horse up and explained everything to them as I laced it up. I told them that, after the fall, there'd be a few inches of cable and the knot attached to the ring. I put them where they would watch the whole thing. Then, after the stunt, I brought the horse over to them and said, "Now check him good." They couldn't find anything wrong with any of the horses we used that day. They said, "If they were all done that way, it'd be all right." But every now and then somebody will cut the price and hurt a horse.'

Despite this demonstration, the Running W and pit falls were eventually outlawed. Since horses still had to make spectacular falls in movies, other methods were needed to make them tumble. These alternatives satisfied American Humane Association officers. But horse handlers and stuntmen considered some of these methods were, ironically, more painful than the older and now-banished techniques. Hal Needham, a horse trainer, as well as a leading stuntman of the 1960s and 1970s, did not care for some systems he sometimes had to use.

'Training a horse to fall on cue is, I think, the most difficult horse stunt there is, because it's so much against his nature. To train a "falling horse" I have to work with him for at least a year, and it isn't until you've used him three or four years that he gets really good. First you tie his leg up with a rope on a pulley, pull his head around very easy and get him to lie down. That way you assure him he isn't going to get hurt. You do this over and over and over.

'Then you do it at a walk; pull his leg with a rope, pull his head around, lay him down. Finally you get to the point where he knows that when you pull his head around you want him to fall. Then you try it out. Sometimes you get lucky and you've got him trained. Other times you wind up thirty feet out in front of the others and they're standing looking at you.

'When you train a "falling horse" you really hurt him in the mouth. I have to put more pressure on his mouth than he gets when he hits the ground. The only reason he falls is that he knows I'm going to hurt him in the mouth if he doesn't. But people who don't know horses don't see that on the screen. They can't know how much abuse that horse has gone through. "Running Ws" can be bad; you can kill a horse with a wire if you try to do it too spectacularly, but the fact that with a Running W you know the exact spot where he'll fall lets you put down eight inches of sand in that place.

'You can also hurt a horse by putting the wire straight out behind him, because he'll turn end over end before he goes down, but if you put it out at a forty-five degree angle he'll turn sideways and go down safely. An animal will take care of himself if you leave him alone. Don't mess with his head, don't try to save him when he hits the end of the cable but let him save himself, and put some sand down for him to land in. I hate anything that's a farce, and that's just what we've got today. The American Humane Association is a pain in the ass.'

Regardless of their impact on the anatomy, vigilant A.H.A. officers were necessary. For some directors and producers the only thing that mattered was to get exciting footage into the cans. Actors and animals were merely expendable pawns in trying to achieve this. If their limbs, or even lives, were imperilled, that's what they were paid for. One action sequence director with a reputation for brutality and callousness was B. Reeves (Breezy) Eason. A pioneer who arrived in Hollywood in 1913, he was a ruthless technician with little thought for the safety of humans or animals in the sequences he shot. He was involved in two famous pictures (the 1925 version of Ben-Hur *and the 1936 version of* The Charge of the Light Brigade*) in which the carnage of horses was notorious.*

Eason's Westerns earned him a reputation for lively action work. This led, logically, to an invitation from M.G.M. in 1925 to shoot the chariot race for its ambitious production of *Ben-Hur*. Already as much a white elephant for M.G.M. as *Cleopatra* was to be for Twentieth Century Fox in the sixties, *Ben-Hur* changed directors and locations at a dizzying rate until Fred Niblo set it back on the rails. Eason, skilled with horse stunts and known for his ability to finish jobs on time and under budget, was an ideal choice for the race. His ruthless methods brought magnificent material, but only at the cost of injured stunt men and dead horses. Estimates of the number of animals killed on the (chariot-race) sequence range as high as 150; rather than treat a maimed horse, it was shot.

. . . It was to Eason that Warners handed the action shooting for *The Charge of the Light Brigade* (1936). Its director was Michael Curtiz, hardest-driving of Warner's staffers, who combined ruthless professionalism with a paradoxically flowing and observant style.

Although he left much of the action to Eason, there is no reason to believe that Curtiz, infamous for his harsh treatment of actors, was unaware of Eason's methods or inclined to criticize them. By wrenching history, the writers began their story in India, getting through a massacre and some desert chases before moving to the Crimea, where Errol Flynn leads his avenging regiment down 'the valley of death' mainly to wipe out the oriental potentate who killed their women and children in India years before. Eason recruited two hundred riders for the India sequences and the charge, and chose from these an elite of thirty-eight stunt horsemen for the major falls and leaps which, intercut with scenes of Flynn leading the attack, made up the charge.

No part of California looked much like India or the Black Sea riviera, so Eason compromised with Sonora in the north of the state, a windy plain below the snow-topped Sierras. But the area was rocky, and his cowboys nervous and angry at having to work without safeguards like sand pits. A man died when, doubling Flynn, he leaped from a high rock onto a rider;

Both movie versions of *Ben-Hur* (1926 and 1959) were rough on the horses needed for the famous chariot race.

Messala (Stephen Boyd) infringing rules of the Rome Equus Club by deliberately crowding his black team against that of Ben-Hur (Charlton Heston). While both actors had months of chariot training, risks for themselves and their horses were high.

the horse shied at the man's shadow and he landed heavily, breaking his neck.

A six-hundred foot trench was driven along one edge of the valley to carry a camera tracking with the riders in low shot, and others cut at right angles across the line of the charge for 'gun pits' and camera emplacements. Since most of the sequence was shot from low angles, countless holes had to be blasted in the flinty rock, and even sand could not soften the jagged edges left by dynamite. Horrific weeks went by, with horses killed and men injured daily, as Eason accumulated the miles of film needed for the 295 fragments of the charge sequence.

Eventually a party from the Glendale Society for the Prevention of Cruelty to Animals visited Sonora. When they filed charges against Warner Brothers, a shocked public heard for the first time what a badly-planned Running W would do. According to a news report, an S.P.C.A. witness stated that the pits were from eight to ten feet deep, but errors in the measurement of the wire caused one animal to dangle helplessly over the edge, its back broken. It was destroyed by employees of the film company. Two other horses had to be killed. According to the same witness, a special pit was prepared to receive the bodies of the injured animals.

Three crew members, including assistant director, J. J. Sullivan, were given miniscule fines, the equivalent of £3.00, but the case dramatized the brutality often inflicted on movie horses. Encouraged, the S.P.C.A. ferreted out other examples. For a scene in Cecil B. de Mille's *Northwest Mounted Police* in 1939 where a Gatling gun is heaved over a cliff into a river, de Mille's second unit director Arthur Rosson set the gun on a rail and had two stunt men riders throw Running Ws on the cliff edge. The stunt men, allegedly well numbed with whisky, were merely bruised; the horses were less lucky. The same year, Twentieth Century Fox, shooting *Jesse James* (Henry King) at the Lake of the Ozarks in Missouri, hired Cliff Lyons for $2,350, a record fee, to jump two horses seventy-five feet into the lake. Since the horses shied in terror from the drop, chutes were built and the animals and rider pushed off. Lyons survived, but both horses were killed. 'What a stink there was over that', he later commented.

The *Jesse James* incident focused growing public indignation at the mistreatment of movie animals. Since 1925, the Association of Motion Picture Producers, Will Hays's self-policing guild, had paid lip service to the principles of humane treatment, but in fact brutality was common. The studios' own humane officers were usually stooges, and though provision existed to call in the S.P.C.A. to supervise animal stunts (at a token $10 a day) this seldom happened.

The proliferation of animal safety organizations also hampered concerted action. As well as local, regional, state and national branches of the S.P.C.A., various local and national Humane Associations were involved. Laws on cruelty to animals were not uniform, but the fact that Missouri had strong legislation allowed the Missouri Humane Association to bring prosecutions against Twentieth Century Fox, a campaign taken up by, among others, Mel Morse, then a minor officer of the Californian S.P.C.A., with a special interest in the problem. When the society refused him paid leave to attend the 1939 American Humane Association convention in Albany, N.Y., he borrowed on his car to make the trip, and put the case for a national policy on animal safety in movies.

A new agreement was negotiated between the Motion Picture Producers Association and the A.H.A. in December 1940, specifically outlawing the Running W and pit fall.

> *These cruelty vigilantes winced and went on the alert in 1959 when M.G.M. announced it would remake* Ben-Hur, *mainly in Italy at Dino de Laurentis's Cinecitta. Yakima Canutt, still arrow-straight but retired as an active stuntman, was hired to supervise the chariot race sequence, months of effort which finally occupied twelve minutes of screen time; his sons, Tap and Joe, did major stunting in the film. Joe Canutt's athleticism and extraordinary reflexes saved his life when Ben-Hur's chariot (Joe was doubling Charlton Heston) got out of control during shooting.*

In the aftermath of *Ben-Hur*, there were inevitable comparisons with the 1925 version and accusations of death and injury during the production. [Second unit director Andrew] Marton, tired of the charges, shocked a press conference by telling them that twenty men had died during the race and a hundred horses. 'That's what you want to hear, isn't it?' he asked angrily, and though most reporters recognized the reproach, his comments fed rumours of hushed-up accidents.

As action films go, *Ben-Hur* was relatively humane. Running Ws were used, and the A.H.A. forced M.G.M. to delete three seconds from a shot of horses collapsing in a crash. A.H.A. executive director Mel L. Morse agrees, 'I have no assurance that any (horses) were actually killed', but adds, 'There certainly was a violation of the Motion Picture Production Code in that wire cables were placed on the animals. I have listened to the stunt men for a period of years telling me that they can do a Running W on a horse and not injure it. If you have ever had the opportunity to see a Running W, you have seen an animal shaken (this is, of course, if the neck isn't broken). The animal will stand trembling for hours afterwards and is usually not fit for anything else after it has been so used. The Motion Picture Production Code wasn't set up just to keep animals from being killed. It was to keep them from being abused.'

This argument is unanswerable. But as long as we, the audience, demand our share of thrills, the stunt men will continue to use these techniques. Blaming them is irrelevant; they are only doing a job. The final moral responsibility is ours.

2 THE HAIRY JOYS OF HANGIN' ON

Dotson Rader

The International Rodeo Association (I.R.A.) is one of two major producing cooperatives that control rodeo in the United States. The I.R.A. sanctions about 350 rodeos a year, most of them small, rural affairs attracting a few thousand spectators each. There are almost 3,000 cowboy members in the I.R.A.; they compete during a rodeo season that lasts from March to January, many of them working on the side, off-season, to support their rodeo careers.

Cowboys begin rodeoing young, usually when they are fifteen or sixteen, and, unless they are badly injured, their careers may last as long as twenty years. They often travel in pairs, a young and an older cowboy together, sharing expenses, living out of beat-up campers or pickup trucks, and driving across the country from one backwater hick town to another trying to gain enough rodeo points to make it once and for all as the World Champion All-Around Cowboy – the cowboy who wins the most rodeo money in two or more events in one year. During a holiday such as the Fourth of July ('the cowboys' Christmas' because so many rodeos are held then) they will compete in as many as six or seven rodeos in four days, driving hundreds of miles between each, going on little sleep and less money, drinking wildcat whisky and surviving on 'crosses', white tabs of amphetamine they buy off long-haul truckers. And when one cowboy is hurt, his partner invariably leaves him, pairs up with someone else, and moves on. The cowboys in the bucking-horse and bull events are usually younger than the others, in their teens or early twenties, and they suffer the most injuries.

The cowboys are mostly Southern or South-eastern, white, and poor. They are, almost without exception, rural in background and, like bull-fighters in Spain, they see the rodeo as the way out, the escape, the ticket into Madison Square or the International Finals in Tulsa where one big win can buy their way to the other side of the steel fence, into the producing or stockman part of the sport. And that's where the money is.

One other thing: rodeo is a rigidly male sport, and it maintains masculine codes of toughness and strength, of winning. And what is unhappy about the cowboys is that they are all aware of the shortness of the time and the wretchedness of the odds against them, and yet they can think of no other option in life.

The Fortieth Annual Wright City, Oklahoma, Rodeo was held on forty acres of cleared piney woods in McCurtain County, west of Idabel, over the Texas line. It was sponsored by the American Legion's William Wright Post.

It was dusk, about a half-an-hour before the rodeo began. It was hot as hell, ninety degrees, the breeze up and dusty, the red, white and blue plastic pennants flapping in the wind over the arena, sounding like ocean waves. The arena was big, and surrounded on three sides by wooden bleachers, red, white and blue. The fourth side held the judges' stand, built over the bull and horse chutes. Behind the chutes were the stock pens, and farther back were parked the cowboys' pickups and campers; near them cowboys were washing themselves down with garden hoses, pulling out their equipment and rigging, and looking over the stock.

The bleachers were two-thirds full, a smaller crowd than the Legion expected. It was very quiet, tension in the air, a heavy stillness except for the snapping pennants. Men and women sat together in the bleachers, fanning themselves, staring straight ahead, very few talking, and even fewer touching each other. The adults drank illegal beer out of white Styrofoam cups as their kids sat beside them in crew cuts or braids, wearing cowboy hats, gripping miniature flags or balloons, waiting for the show to begin.

Legion Post Commander Arzie Elliott stood by the ticket shack waving people in. A World War II veteran, wearing his blue Legion service cap, the bottom edges wet with sweat, his belly hanging over his belt. 'I *never* seen no boy killed. Hell, but last week in Texas a boy got killed. And I seen a boy's back broke. I think up there in Cheyenne. Bull stepped on this boy's back and broke it like a matchstick. I seen 'em kicked in the head, all over the place.'

Below the judges' stand about thirty nervous young cowboys paced on the platform between the stock pens and the chutes. They had each paid twenty-five dollars per event to compete in the rodeo, and for that they bought the chance of being ground by a bull into the arena's red river clay, or, one of them, winning a $600 top. The rodeo profits are always divided between the producer and the sponsoring organization.

I introduced myself to Jim Hill, twenty-four, from Union City, Tennessee, who has hazel eyes deep-set in a lean, rough-complexioned face and a wide gap-toothed smile. The judges had drawn stock lots. Hill pointed out the bull he had drawn. A huge black Brahma bull.

12

'I've seen him go. He's a mean bastard.'

Hill jumped off the stand to the ground and slapped the bull's rump through the fence to make him stand. The bull snorted and then suddenly stood up, glaring at Hill and pawing the dirt.

'See,' he said, 'he's got a long back, which means he's long and fast. I seen him do one or two jumps and turn right on his ass, scoot his butt around in a tight circle instead of kicking. He'll shoot you over his butt, see. I seen him dive.'

Hill spoke laconically, his voice a soft drawl. His nose was scarred from being hooked by a bull two years before. He was wearing a black stetson with a feather in its band.

'Are you scared?'

He grinned. 'My motor's running.' He stared again at the bull. 'Bad mother. Never drawn him before. I seen him hook up a couple fellas. Jack Wiseman, world champion, rode him in Detroit city. He's a mean mother. Quiet, ain't he? When they're quiet like that they *know*. They're resting up to hook ya.'

He slugged the fence. The bull flinched and snorted.

'Do you think you'll get hooked?' An awkward question; Hill ignored it.

'A bull's more aggressive than a horse. A horse will avoid hurtin' ya or stepping on ya once you're thrown. But a bull? They wanna kill ya. A green bull will hunt out a throwed cowboy.'

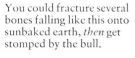

You could fracture several bones falling like this onto sunbaked earth, *then* get stomped by the bull.

'Then why ride them?'

He rubbed his nose. 'I love it, the life. 'Bout the only free one left . . . I get a feelin' of conquerin' an animal. You ride a tough animal and you can feel 'em between your legs. You wrap your thighs around 'em and their muscles and your muscles sort of talk. That's where the fight is, *here*.' Hill bent his knees slightly and thrust his hands under his crotch, gripping his upper thighs. 'See,' he smiled, 'they say it's like sex, but it isn't. It's better.'

By the pens, Hill began preparing his rigging and dressing for his bull. With him was Tony Coleman, his partner, a skinny kid in a black stetson and black rimmed glasses, who stood at the side with a chaw of Skoal tobacco between his lower lip and teeth.

Hill opened his rigging bag, a large, black canvas sack with his name stencilled in white on it. He pulled out his bull rope, a plaited rope fifteen feet long with a stiff leather handle braided into it halfway along its length. The rope had an adjustable loop on one end and a narrow tail at the other. The rope is placed around the bull's midsection so that the handle sticks up from the animal's back. The tail is drawn through the loop and then wrapped around the rider's hand as it grasps the handle. Next, Hill took out his bull glove, a long-cuffed goatskin glove hardened with benzoin. He tried it on. Then he took two large cowbells that he attached to the rope and which would ride under the belly of the bull during the bucking event. When the rider is thrown clear, if he is lucky and his hand isn't trapped in the glove or by the wrapped rope, the weight of the bells will pull his rope and rigging off the bull. And then there was a horsehair pad that fits under the rider's hand; a set of long shanked spurs with long, five-point rowels to dig into and grip the bull's side. Finally Hill drew out a strip of foam rubber.

A bull rider sits on the backbone of the animal, at its middle, and to protect the base of their spines, cowboys shove a foam-rubber strip in their trouser bottoms. They wear especially tight jeans and no athletic cup; they try to protect their genitals by shoving them up and over their left thigh, where the tight pant leg will usually hold their sex snugly in place above the bull's back.

Also in Hill's rigging bag were his bareback rigging, rosin, talcum powder, saddle soap, extra wire, leather pliers, screwdriver, an old knife, a bottle of benzoin, tape, and Ace wraps.

Hill 'strung his tack' (hung his equipment on the corral fence) and checked it through to make sure it was rosined up and ready to use. Then he did some groin stretching and back bending. 'The important muscles is the riding arm and the neck. It's the neck that takes the beating. Bull ridin' is a hard event. Bulls buck so much different from horses. Got a shorter, stouter, rollin' buck to them. You have to take short, choppy, uneven holds.

Just before the rodeo began, Hill suited up, pulling on his spurs and chaps, and trying on the glove.

We climbed up to the platform under the judges' stand and stood by the bucking chutes. Hill lit a Marlboro, opening the pack at the bottom, a habit he picked up in Vietnam. And then he stood a moment and went into a kind of movieland cowboy pose; that is, he stood grinning by the bucking chute, his face pink in the late evening light, dressed in his fancy black and white chaps, his black boots and stetson with feather, cigarette at the side of his mouth, his left hand feeling the prized cowboy buckle he had won in an unsanctioned show, his right hand resting against his hipbone. In about ten minutes he would mount the bull in chute number two – one of five bulls kicking and banging against the steel chutes, waiting for their riders and release. Excrement oozed from the bulls' behinds, its odour mingling with smells of urine and the pine woods and the cowboys' Old Spice and beer breath.

'How do you feel now?' I asked Hill.

He drew on his cigarette, and shifted his weight from one foot to the other. He tapped his hat back on his head and lowered his eyebrows. He touched his nose. 'Well, I got this chargin' feeling. I want get to it, away from it. Maybe I wanna ride. What am I doin' here? Mixed emotion, a lot, and I'm borne up on concentrating on doin' things right and proper, and I want to get over that box (chute) and it's me and him, you know. I come to do my thing. Bull, you do yours. We both got to make a livin'.'

'You know, in a minute, when I get down on him I get a confident feelin'. It's kinda a defiant feeling, more or less the challenge has been answered. I think a rodeo bull's beautiful, as beautiful an animal as ever lived. Enjoyable and rough. You got this bolt of power that keeps snatchin' at you, bitin', jerkin', at you. It's constant fight to keep the mother from stringin' you out. You're grabbin' air, pullin' for life . . .'

Hill paused and took off his hat. He scratched his head. 'No, I guess not. I guess I hold my breath all the time I'm there ridin'. Tense like a coiled spring on that bull. I run a hundred yards. I sweat crazy. All that tension bleedin' out when it's through. You're dry, and then it's over, and *hissst!* the waterfall rolls over you, the sweat comes, all the tension breaks, see, it breaks.'

The Washington Post march sounded out over the loudspeakers and seventy mounted riders poured in parade into the arena, old men in service caps or stetsons, riding quarter horses, carrying American Legion, national, Ladies Auxiliary, and Oklahoma state flags . . . girls in white blouses on paints . . . a pony waggon . . . beauty queens from Ada and Golden, 'The Honey Pot of the World'. The crowd cheered. It was beginning.

'Welcome to the Fortieth Annual Wright City Rodeo brought to you by William Wright American Legion Post, by patriotic American Legions families who gave time, toil, labour, sweat . . . Pure good ol' American, civil-minded, America-minded, club-minded vets who contributed time and efforts to bring you the very best rodeo, stock and professional cowboys

who might win a small fortune (the $600) if they out-rope, out-ride, out-buck, out-win the competition . . . '

The crowd applauded, good feelings rising in anticipation of the opening chutes. The announcer changed the tape on the Masterwork tape deck and *The Star-Spangled Banner* blared out; the riders fell into studied formation, the people stood, the cowboys took off their hats and held their hands over their hearts, and when it was over they cheered. And then a Deep Water Baptist preacher gave a long, very long, invocation asking the Lord Jesus to let the best man win and save the souls of the lost and disconsolate. The cowboys stood with their heads bowed as the preacher prayed and the bulls banged restlessly in the chutes and fireflies played over the grass in the pasture behind the pens.

In a moment Jim Hill would mount his bull. Before he did he stood by the pens, his back to the other men, and relieved himself. Then he carefully arranged his crotch.

'I'm anxious over what's comin' on,' he said. And with that he pulled on his bull glove. He climbed over onto the top of chute two. Cowboys gathered around. He rested his boot heels on the chute fence on either side of the black animal, balancing himself with his hand on the top railing. With his free hand he adjusted his rigging, and then he shoved his gloved hand into the braided handle, bent the hard hand over the handle and waited as the rope was wound over his glove and the topes tightened, around the bull. He crossed himself, looked up and smiled.

The announcer called out his name. The music stopped. The rodeo clown, whose job it is to distract the bull away from a thrown rider, positioned himself in the arena. His was the most dangerous task.

Hill tightened his hand. He straightened his arm out hard. He gritted his teeth and stared down at the bull, shifting his body subtly in response to the motion of the bull, lowering himself slowly onto the animal, leaning forward as he did, cautiously, responsively, awake to every reaction. The bull made a bucking motion and then settled down. Hill lifted his free hand, signalling the gateman. The chute flew open.

The crowd murmured; the cowboys leaned forward over the railings, their bodies moving instinctively with the movement of man and bull suddenly thrust into the arena. The bull bucked twice, and Hill was flung to the right, still holding on, and then breaking; he was thrown back over the bull, his body missing by inches the back of the bull's hooves. Hill landed hard in the clay and the bull swivelled toward him, head lowered. The clown intervened, the bull twisted toward him, for a moment hesitating as if confused about which way to charge. But he hesitated long enough, giving Hill the time to scamper to the railing and over it, his face white, sweat pouring like a waterfall over his face, his breathing laboured, his face taut. He had escaped.

Jim Hill was thrown in five seconds. A rider has to remain on the animal a minimum of eight to win. He had lost.

Nine other young bull riders followed. None was hurt. None won. All lost money.

And then the clown told some dirty jokes and the crowd laughed. The mood relaxed. People got up and moved around, and the drinking began to get serious in the bleachers, and the first fist fights broke out behind the stands.

Other events followed; calf roping; the calf scramble (kids' event); another clown act; steer wrestling; bareback riding; a specialty act; a barrel race (women); the clown again.

The audience had lost interest, and it was late. People were moving out, heading for the dance on the other side of the arena gates where for three dollars they could two-step to Ferlin Husky and Conway Twitty records under a forty-watt light; heading for that and for the illegal whiskey and beer waiting in car coolers. The sports tension has gone from the rodeo, replaced by a different, meaner one, that of spectators at rural events, of the guys who sit on their butts beside the little woman in the bleachers watching the younger men compete as most of them never have. A kind of bitterness and resentment comes over them, and they start cursing the cowboys and jazzing the clown. They start showing off.

Before the dance was over, Jim Hill and Tony Coleman got in their old Ford pickup with its bumper sticker 'Keep the Old West Alive – Ball a Cowboy', and they headed toward Missouri, twenty hours away, to compete in another rodeo.

3 CRACKING COLDIES AT THE BIRDSVILLE RACES

Rex Ellis

During one Birdsville race meeting, I stood at night on the first of the Simpson Desert sandhills at the edge of town. The whole scene appeared and sounded unreal. At my back, four hundred miles of silence and loneliness; in front of me the tiny township bursting with noise and lights.

Rex Ellis

Like Alice Springs, Birdsville is one of the near-fabled towns of the Australian outback. For this book we are concerned with its two-day picnic race meeting, held in the first week of each September. This race meeting is unique. Wildly, boozily, colourfully, gloriously unique – an extraordinary piece of Australiana. Many readers in other lands will know little of Birdsville (sadly, an overlong list of lazy Australians are as ignorant of it). So, it will pay to sketch in some background of town and race meeting to allow greater understanding of Mr Ellis's magnificent chronicle of one cup meeting.

Mr Ellis tells us that Birdsville came into being around the late 1870s. Two theories have grown about the origin of its name. The first (which Mr Ellis accepts) is that a man named Burt set up a store on one of the permanent waterholes there on the Diamentina River. Previously he had run a store from a place known as Burt's Hole about sixty miles south of Birdsville near Goyder's Lagoon swamp. But water here was not permanent. At his new location, Burt catered for growing numbers of drovers moving their fat channel-country cattle south to markets at Adelaide. From its original name of Burtsville, the theory goes, the lazy Australian tongue slurred it into Birdsville. The second theory is straightforward: permanent waterholes meant abundant birdlife, rare in these desert regions, and so . . .

Whatever the truth, Birdsville expanded into a customs post in the thirty years until Federation in 1901. It is a border township, just six miles into Queensland above the South Australian border and about seventy miles west of the Northern Territory border; Alice Springs lies some 360 miles west-northwest. In early days

More like a wild west chase than a flat race; horses negotiate a bend on a wild part of the course.

drovers paid about sixpence per sheep and a shilling a head of cattle to move stock across the state border. The town boasted three pubs, a soft drink factory and the usual cluster of government buildings; a bustling community for the outback. In fact, that region had more people in it seventy years ago than now. But life was cruelly hard. Infant mortality was very high because no medical attention was at hand – a setback the Flying Doctor service later remedied. Summer temperatures that could climb to 124°F. (51°C.) in mid-summer (mercifully with nil humidity) meant mental and physical oppression. Fatalism could set in, as shown in a two-sentence entry in a police diary, dated February 2, 1904: 'Constable Brown shot himself on the front verandah this morning. Another hot day'. Drought, along with such things as cattle prices, has expanded and contracted the township's population down the years. Drought means a countryside denuded of herbage and animals, of scraggy, withered perennial trees and shrubs (and the picnic races cancelled because local horses have been too poorly to run). It also brings duststorms that can rage for days. When they are over, the residents – usually the women – have had to clear their dwellings of dust and sand, often by the shovelful. When good seasons come (as in 1972–76, the best spell on record), the whole country comes to life. Sandhills become a riot of herbage and wild flowers: poached egg daisies, everlastings, wild parsnip, yellow bud, tall yellow top, Sturt's desert pea and so on. River flats and flood plains are covered in a green herbage with a blue flower, growing so tall (up to seven feet) cattle and horsemen can disappear in it.

In the mid-1970s Birdsville's population (which does float a lot) was around fifty people, most of whom were part or full aboriginal; of the twenty-three pupils at the state school, only four were white. Most of the men worked for the local Diamentina Shire Council, or on surrounding stations. So the breadwinner, and his whole family, could be away for months.

The famous pub was founded about 1885, operating, like most pioneer country pubs, as a 'grog shanty'.

Race meetings, which were not registered, began, it is thought, in the early 1890s; origins are hazy. Organizers chose the early Spring to take advantage of the best weather of the year: average day temperatures 75–80°F (24–27°C.) with no humidity; balmy nights; conditions most conducive to quick recovery from hangovers. In pre-motoring days, stalwarts would journey on horseback from stations two hundred miles away. They would have two hacks, perhaps two racehorses and sometimes rest the hacks by riding a racehorse. They could be away from home for three weeks: one week travelling there, a week in Birdsville, a week for the return journey. Stringy, sun-dried bushmen still turn up there. They are an old-fashioned, yet strangely solid presence amid the sleek city businessmen, salesmen, big-spread farmers and graziers who wing in aboard their private aircraft.

The Birdsville race meeting has always belonged to these resolute and uncomplicated people. No matter what layers of imported gloss are introduced, it always will.

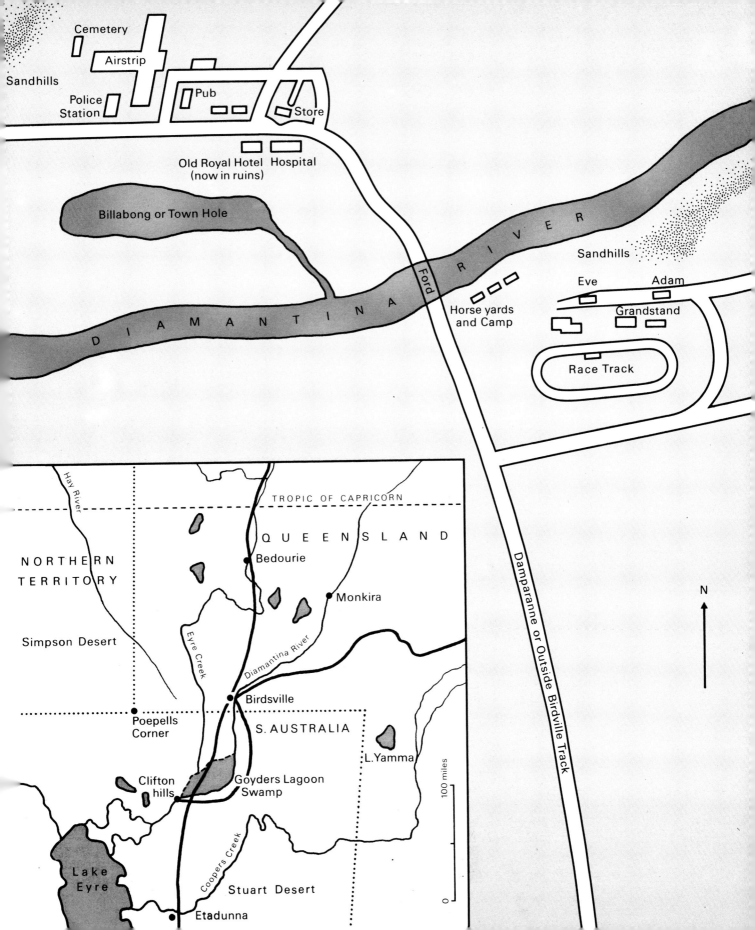

The old ex-army blitz truck growled its way to the top of a sandhill. After the crest, its metal nose dipped to reveal stretched before us the timber-clad flood plains of the Diamentina River. On the far side of the main channel lay our destination – the tiny outpost of Birdsville perched on a stony rise between the Diamentina and the yellow and red void of the Simpson Desert.

I own the Birdsville pub and travel there each September for the Picnic Race meeting, a two-day event famous throughout Australia. These days it is, by our sense of tradition, a very cosmopolitan affair. The bulk of the crowds are still outback station people but a large assortment of dedicated racegoers come from all parts of Australia. Some arrive in aircraft, some in trucks and sedans (some set out but don't arrive at all). My means of travel include aeroplane and truck.

This year (1975) I had flown from Adelaide on an oil company aircraft to the Moomba Gas Fields, where I met up with Kevin McCarthy of Gidgealpa Station, a 'battler's' block located on the banks of famed Cooper Creek.

My business is outback safaris and I stay at Gidgealpa two or three times a year. On my last visit Kevin had told me he planned to travel cross-country to the races in his four-wheel-drive blitz truck; he thought his horse Sandstorm was ripe for the Birdsville meeting.

So, Wednesday morning was an antheap of movement as eleven adults and kids loaded swags (sleeping bags), chaff, oats, glad rags (best clothes) and meat supply – half a bullock – onto the blitz. Sandstorm was hustled from the relative comfort of his stable to his somewhat spartan two-wheel trailer hooked up behind the truck. During the hundred miles cross country journey to the Birdsville track, as the trailer bumped across crab-hold flats and gibber plains, through gullies and over sandhills, Sandstorm had a condensed pre-race workout.

We reached the Birdsville track about eight p.m. that day and drove along searching for the right terrain – a gutter or high ground we could back the truck up to and lead the horse easily from the trailer. After many miles of dead flat, we came across a large sandhill known locally as 'Deadman'. It was here in the early part of the century that three horsemen had perished. Five stockmen, riding back to Inamencka from a Birdsville race meeting, had an argument about the right route to follow. The party split up, two taking the correct route home; the other three rode south to die on the 'Deadman'. In the final stages of dehydration, they desperately slashed their horses' throats and drank the blood.

We had our own lesser problems there. We chose a three-foot-high sand hump, planning to drive the blitz hard at it and stop dead when the rear of the horse trailer had crossed it and come back down level. But we bogged in the soft sand and had to heave what seemed like a mountain of sand with shovels until we had enough flattened to make an unloading ramp. While all this was going on, the women were cooking steak; soon we settled down for a beer and a meal. Then swags were rolled out after a long day.

Early next morning, we unbogged the truck, loaded *Sandstorm* and continued on up the track to Birdsville. As I mentioned earlier, some never reach there. In 1974, driving a Range Rover north along the track to the race meeting, I came across two Melbourne racegoers whose two-wheel Ford Falcon had bogged in the mud. We didn't have the motor power in the slimy-wet conditions to get them out; so we drove on. Three days later we met them again, a mile north of their previous position. They had unbogged their car, gone the mile then bogged again. We gave them food, some cans of beer, the race results and left them once more. Those who drive four-wheel vehicles enjoy their journey to Birdsville, giving it roaring overtones of a motor rally. As always, getting there, then back home again, can bring much of the fun.

At race time, Birdsville is split into two main areas of activity – the pub and the racecourse, a mile apart, with the Diamentina River running between (see map). A concrete causeway spans the river but in this first week of September – early Spring for us – the Diamentina is shrunken to a string of waterholes. Along the river on the racecourse side are sets of horse yards made from coolibah timber. We chose one of these and in no time had set up a bush camp, an activity duplicated all around us as more trucks arrived with horses. A truck carrying four horses bogged close to our camp. Kevin drove his blitz over and pulled it out. The truck had tilted so dangerously the horses had to be prodded to leap down from the rear – a ticklish procedure that would give Jockey Club stewards elsewhere an attack of the fits. After checking that Sandstorm lacked for nothing in his new home we drove across the river to the pub.

The Birdsville pub is famous for many reasons. It is the focal point of this town which is literally a speck in the middle of nowhere. It is this remoteness and relative inaccessibility (even today) that help to make the Birdsville races unique. Although most of them have never been there, or would want to live there, urban Australians identify with the vast outback of their immense country. I feel that a great many people, thousands of miles away, harbour a soft spot for Birdsville and are proud of it: they look upon it as a frontier outpost. So, while very few Australians (relatively) have been to Birdsville, thousands would recognise a photograph or painting of the country's most isolated pub. A ninety-year-old ramshackle building made from local stone and painted a defiant red and white, it is the mecca for outback tourists. I have seen people tiptoe into its bar as reverently as they would into St Paul's Cathedral or up to the Mona Lisa in the Louvre. The pub is the 'local' for a few hundred people scattered over a vast area; its walls have soaked up some of Australia's tallest tales; many of the more lurid, humorous and scandalous of these have been swapped at race time.

I went around the bar and said g'day to Taffy and Sylvie Nicholls. They run the pub for me and do a really good job. We knocked the tops off a round of stubbies (pint-sized bottles of beer) and settled down for a bar-keeping marathon of seventy-two hours.

During this period the pub would remain virtually unclosed, except for a couple of hours each morning on Friday and Saturday (the race days) and Sunday (recuperation and farewells) when bar and 'lounge' are cleaned up. This is no small job, as you'll learn later. The pub throbs with activity from Thursday evening to Sunday evening. At least one third of the annual turnover is scooped in during these three days and nights. In 1974 we sold ten tons of beer during the race meeting. In 1975 the 700 people who invaded the township gulped down ten tons of beer, $3\frac{1}{2}$ tons of soft drinks, 15 bottles of Scotch whisky, 25 dozen bottles of Bundaberg (Queensland) rum and a cataract of more arcane tipples. There is no draught beer on tap, therefore no kegs. Beer is sold in 370mm. cans and those glass stubbies that fit nicely into the hand.

The township boasts no restaurant or cafe; just the pub and store. In earlier years an imported caterer used to move into the pub kitchen for the race meeting. But he ran the risk of being bogged in transit, having the meeting rained off and thus losing thousands of dollars. In 1975 the Nichollses catered: breakfast and lunch about $2 Aust; dinner, $3:00 – pay at the door and eat in the pub dining room. This arrangement piled a second mountain of cooking and washing-up work on top of the already frenetic pubkeeping. Hawkers also turn up for the meeting. There is usually one large van parked opposite the pub and selling such items as jeans, khaki and checked shirts, riding boots to the stockmen. Business thrives.

By three p.m. on the Thursday, a dozen light aircraft were already parked on the strip not far from the bar window, the advance flock of the fifty-five planes that will touch down throughout the meeting. The airstrip is strategic: pilots and passengers have to walk only a hundred yards from cockpit to bar rail. Laughing newcomers join the bar crowd of some twenty people, mostly local aborigines, stockmen and council workers, with a sprinkling of tourists. The first light aircraft began to appear in the early 1950s, led by Jack Clancy, a pioneer plane owner among 'locals'. Jack used to fly down from Cooraboulka Station 190 miles to the north east. The first year six planes turned up, including the Flying Doctor, who usually finds an excuse to be there for the races. Actually the pub caters year round for air travellers. Trans Australia Airways operates a weekly flight through Birdsville from Brisbane to Alice Springs: arrive westbound at Birdsville Saturdays, and back from Alice on Sunday afternoons en route for Brisbane. During the half-hour stopover, passengers amble to the pub for a drink. Teetotallers can grab a quick look through the store owned by Bill and David Brook, father and son. Curiously and most unusually, the store is part of Adria Downs Station, whose homestead is right in the middle of the township.

Around four-thirty p.m. on our race eve, in trooped four of my mates. These iron men were going to help behind the bar throughout the meeting. Like all the others, they brought an air of excitement and anticipation. We exercised our wrists beheading stubbies until the dinner gong at seven o'clock urged some drinkers into the dining room and others back to their camps. Afterwards a large crowd, mostly aborigines and children, went off to see the Buddy Williams Show featuring a Country and Western outfit well known throughout Australia.

Thursday night before the races is really a warm-up, a throat-loosener and arm-flexer. It slid by so jovially that suddenly it was three a.m. and we were firmly coaxing the last diehard revellers out into the night. Taffy and I then locked up. This was a gesture because a ringer (stockman) – thirst-crazed I imagine – had once tried to run through the closed door, splitting it right down the middle. We locked what remained of it and went to our various beds. I didn't have far to go; my swag was spread out behind the bar. The pub is booked out months ahead for the race meeting. We end up with forty people, or more, sleeping under the roof of the sixteen-bed pub. Just because I own the Birdsville Pub doesn't mean I can get a bed there at race time. That was my last waking thought.

At six-thirty a frantic scratching at the door wakened me. Ten minutes of lying still and willing it to go away were in vain. So I dragged myself from the swag and opened the door. On the doorstep stood a seedy individual in a large bush hat, desperate-eyed and pleading for a cold, life-sustaining stubbie. I took pity and let him in. But, after locking the door I knew my sleeping was through; I grabbed the broom and plunged into the debris that had been the bar. Taffy arrived soon after and it took us an hour to restore things for the Friday assault.

We had already served a stream of various gaspers and stubbie wheedlers before the busted door swung open officially at ten o'clock. By eleven the bar was packed. We spotted many stayers from the previous day and night looking surprisingly spruce and alert; the Cup adrenalin was boosting them along.

Through the bar window we could see planes regularly dropping down, then taxiing to their parking points at the boundaries of the strip. Many parked aircraft had tents alongside them. Under some wings were stretched lumpen swags whose occupants slept through the roar of revving and sputtering motors. Among those mobile and greeting old friends was Kevin McCarthy, hobbling in an outlandish pair of plastic shoes, a major concession the normally-barefoot Kevin was making to the social graces of the Cup meeting.

Just before lunch we began to load cartons of beer and spirits and other drink into the back of an old army Studebaker car to take to the 'booth' at the racecourse. Especially equipped for safaris into the Simpson Desert, this car does fine hack work carting grog (liquor) and racegoers the two miles from town to course. When booze and some twenty assorted passengers were aboard, we cranked the engine and careered off to the course amid much yelling from kids and barking of dogs.

The 'booth' at the course is very basic and uncomplicated – just a bough shed with a spinifex-thatched roof. Rough rails run along three sides, supporting a two-foot-wide board that serves as the bar. At the rear we hang a tarpaulin from the roof; it serves as carport for the Studebaker and coolstore for beer and spirits. The cash register is an old biscuit tin placed on a table next to the spirits and cigarettes. Water for the spirits comes from a water bag slung from the roof; we fill the bag from a water truck. We have no refrigeration but we believe the beer keeps pretty cold under tarpaulins on the truck. Many drinkers dispute this; complaints about warm beer are like a constant musak in the background. One of the fondest Australian habits is to moan about the temperature of the beer; our barmen give stock answers ('It's not as warm as your missus'; 'You'll get a cold drink in Adelaide; it's just down the road') and get on with their work. The Studebaker ferries fresh supplies from the pub all afternoon.

The racing? Ah yes, it does take place. And for competing owners it's a very important business. They tend to mask their competitiveness under broad grins and rowdy mateship, but it can be very keen between old rivals. For some who live in such a harsh and demanding environment, almost everything in life has a barb of challenge in it. Yet, for most, the outing itself is what counts: the reunion with old mates; the swapped yarns; the pleasure of companionship – perhaps the only time in the whole year – for people mostly starved of it; a few women preening their new fashions; later the whoop-up at the dance. In the early 1970s we brought in merry-go-rounds and some sideshows to spark a carnival atmosphere.

On Friday, the first day, there are four or five races between one-thirty and around five o'clock. Average fields are six to eight horses, some of which are local and others imported for the big meeting. It was back in 1938 that a local station owner, Celsey Morton, first brought up horses from Adelaide to race against the local horses. Riders are either lightweight locals, usually stockmen, or imported professional jockeys who have been competing since 1955. However, we do get races with only three or four runners. These are an easy job for the race commentator, who was introduced in 1974 to give the meeting a further touch of Flemington, or Epsom, class. These races are so easy in fact, the commentator has boiled his billy for a fresh brew of tea between the start and finish, a sight that has the crowd hooting with glee. This especially tickles those who have seen more sophisticated racing, but it is one more part of the rough charm of the Birdsville meeting.

The wild location of the Birdsville races does not diminish the popularity of the annual meeting.

Anticipation and suspense among the Birdsville crowd.

The main race, the Birdsville Cup, is run on the Saturday. It carries $500 Aust. prize money, plus a handsome silver cup. Because it's the big event, excitement and anticipation builds up on the Friday and throughout Saturday morning. Yet the fizz quickly dies: because the Cup usually has no more than three or four runners, it's no dramatic spectacle. But it is the high point of our social year so it's held in great affection.

There are racegoers who have been coming for years and who have never seen even a single racehorse, let alone a race. Their priority is what comes out of their glass or stubbie. Throughout the afternoon on both days, the booth is either teeming or almost deserted (for up to five minutes as the *sportsmen* drift to the rails to watch the next race). Those who keep us constant company are the hard core of dedicated drinkers and inebriates who don't, or can't, make the rail. They are wise not to stir: the pounding rush back to the booth after each race would endanger their lives.

Towards mid-afternoon crowds are almost as thick around the caterer's caravan where a sweating staff dispenses pies, pasties, sandwiches, sausage rolls and so on. The caravan is well placed, right behind the 'grandstand', another bough shelter with plank seats. Further along is the jockey's changing room and secretary's office, neither of which is in line for an architectural award. Behind these buildings and right at the foot of the sandhills are ladies and gents toilets marked with large black letters: EVE and ADAM; not unique labelling but somehow fitting. This group of rough structures and the track itself are all set in a large claypan at the foot of a thirty-five-foot off-white sandhill. While outback folk tend to talk and move slowly the whole scene during the racemeeting is a steady churn of people moving from booth, rail, caterer's caravan, bookies' stands and, very importantly, to those toilets on the sandhills. Now and then movement becomes agitated when a skirmish breaks out near the booth. These rarely develop into brawls but, when tempers cool, can bring new testiness as the near-combatants begin to argue as to who will buy the first drink.

When the last race on Friday is run, the crowd head back to town or to nearby stations to spruce themselves up for the dance. We load the Studebaker with remnants of the stock, place the banknote-choked tin on the front seat and chug the car, decorated with assorted racegoers, back to the pub. By the time we get back, the crowd is spilling out of doorways and windows onto the street. I'm the owner but have to hack and barge my way through the pack while clutching biscuit tin and cartons.

Inside, on one side is the main bar, an area twenty feet by ten feet. Behind it is an uneven gash in the wall, labelled the Green Lizard Bar. Further down the same wall a swinging half door makes a second entrance to the 'lounge', a large room whose wrought iron tables and chairs look out of place; rough planking would look more the thing. At one corner of the lounge is a cold room and at the back a door leading into the bulk beer and liquor store.

The lay-out is hardly perfect: barmen have to crash their way through packed drinkers to reach the store room then plough back laden with cartons.

When the dance gets under way in the hall, a galvanised-iron building, about nine-o'clock on Friday night, it mercifully thins out the hotel crowd. In early years, dress at the dance was almost entirely formal. Men in dress suits and women in long gowns whirled to a local make-shift 'orchestra' of squeezebox and piano. Nowadays a three-or-four-piece band, often with vocalist, flies or drives into town to perform. Sartorial standards have loosened. Older people still prefer their formal wear (after all, this is their big gala night of the year). We also see a smattering of lounge suits and street frocks looking oddly old-fashioned among the youth in shorts, tee-shirts and thong sandals. Women take the evening seriously; most still choose long gowns.

Everyone mixes well and enters into the spirit of the event. Sometimes in an unusual way. One year several of us, walking between pub and hall, saw a young couple trotting down the street hand-in-hand. Nothing remarkable about that except . . . . they where stark naked. News spread like wildfire. Within seconds every exit in pub and hall was blocked with people trying to scramble through. Drunks who came spilling out into the street, glasses in hand, rushed after the quietly perambulating pair. Suddenly they went into top gear and vanished into the darkness followed by a chorus of whistles and cheers. It seems they had lost most of their money at a dice game. Another gambler jokingly suggested they would take up a collection if the couple performed a streak down the main street. Almost instantly the couple had stripped bare, had a seventy dollar collection in their hands and were on their way.

The dance usually dissolves about three o'clock. And an hour later most of the pub crowd has wandered off to beds or swags, wherever they might be. The Stayers linger, some with heads asleep on the bar, others just as bright and wide awake as they were a day and a half ago. The exhausted barmen struggle on. As a rule by about seven a.m. the last patron, usually protesting, is ushered through the door, which is quickly locked and bolted. Now begins the cleaning up by the next group of barmen, who have grabbed a few hours' sleep.

Confronting them is the routine Birdsville drinking aftermath, which suggests Hurricane Bertha has just passed through town. Floors are a mass of empty cans and stubbie bottles and treacherous underfoot from spilt beer. Every flat surface – bar, table tops, window ledges, mantelpiece – is chock-a-block with empty cans. Barmen scoop up the refuse with shovels and toss it into a dozen forty-four gallon drums waiting on the verandah; a shire council truck will collect the full drums later in the day. When the hard debris is gone and the floor visible once more, the mop brigade moves in for the final clean-up; by nine o'clock the pub is ready for the Saturday onslaught.

Somehow the Saturday morning crowd seems in greater fettle than the previous day; perhaps their constitutions are hardening with experience. Much of the talk is about the Cup race. Though some are showing signs of strain, the whole crowd exudes good fellowship, which is one of the real delights of this annual fiesta. I have a quick drink with Kevin McCarthy, who is disappointed about Sandstorm's performance the day before. After his epic journey across the gibber plains, the horse went lame in the first race and couldn't compete in any others. This bad luck has not diminished Kevin's cheerfulness.

At the course, the crowd is bigger, more planes and cars having arrived that morning. The claypan throbs with life. One exuberant pilot lands his Cessna light aircraft on the middle of the track and takes off again before the Clerk of the Course can ride over and make a formal protest. Each race is marked by a great chorus of cheers that billows through the crowd as the horses pound down the home straight and past the winning post.

After the final race a crowd, almost entirely of men, gathers around the booth. A shifty-eyed man appears and produces kip and two pennies; a game of Australia's distinctive and illegal 'two-up' is about to get under way. The pennies glint as they spin through the air and banknotes zip back and forth among the circle of bettors.

As I came up to the Studebaker, clutching the inevitable biscuit tin, I found it being used as a portable grandstand by a dozen or so gamblers; they were hanging over the side above the two-up ring and waving fivers and tenners. We had to return to the pub straight away. There was no way I could coax them off the truck. So I hit the starter button and the truck leapt away in a cloud of dust. Some men tumbled off. Others clung to the vehicle, bellowing fruity comments at the back of my neck. I shouted that I was saving them money. By the time we reached the pub curses had changed to laughter.

We now launched into our busiest stint of barkeeping. Every order, every question, every instruction had to be shouted to rise above the unabating din. We worked on, serving drinks, changing money, talking people out of fights and, hardest of all, ploughing through the morass of people en route to the bulk beer supply.

On one such expedition, Greg, a barman, was unwittingly caught up in an interlude that would have fitted perfectly into the off-duty shenanigans of boisterous cavalrymen in a John Ford western. Greg battled manfully to the coldroom where he almost became the first man in Birdsville history to go down with frostbite: some joker kept him locked inside for five minutes. He was coming back, moving like a slow bulldozer through a forest, with a carton of beer cans under each arm, when a fight broke out in a corner of the room. As always happens, the crowd fell back to give the fighters punching room. Such was the press of humanity that sections of the crowd toppled over into threshing heaps. Greg finished up like cheese spread in a sandwich: lying atop one layer of drinkers with more layers on top of him. But he valiantly kept clutching the cartons. As he lay quietly suspended, waiting for the fight to subside a muffled voice eddied up from beneath his left armpit: 'Hey, mate, any chance of cracking a coldie. The service is bloody lousy down this way'. Somehow the fellow prised a bottle from the carton, Greg got its top off (with an opener) and passed it down to the drinker doing temporary service as a carpet. He gurgled it down happily. A few moments later the fight ended – both combatants were removed horizontal – and Greg scrambled up to resume his return journey to the bar.

And so the night bubbled along with time losing all significance. At midnight we shouted: 'a drink for the bar'. A big cheer at this. Soon afterwards, celebration champagne was sloshed into the Birdsville Cup. The winning owner and his friends chug-a-lugged this down their throats and shirtfronts. Then, above the laughter and shouts, came a single dull thud: Mick the Simpson Desert fencer had fallen off his stool for the third time. He usually stayed down below bar level for a half hour or so, and then re-appeared, looking amazingly fresh and ready for another beer.

Right through to four o'clock the bar crowd held packed and lively. All this time the dance throbbed on, finally winding up just before five o'clock, when the band couldn't raise another note. At this stage harmony was transferred to the pub. Taffy brought out his squeezebox and a guitar or two appeared. Out boomed a big chorus of accompanying voices, not one of them getting within half the scale of proper key and pitch.

I managed to sneak off to my swag at five o'clock. When I reappeared at seven-thirty, the tableau was as the day before: Hurricane Bertha had made an encore. Smashed glasses, prostrate cans and bottles smothered the entire shiny-wet floor area. The only occupant of the lounge was a very distinguished grey-haired gentleman dressed in tails. He was sitting slumped at one of the wrought-iron tables, asleep, with a half-finished Scotch in front of him. In the bar Taffy was arguing vigorously with an agitated Queenslander about the possibilities of straining barbed wire through a fence post rather than around it. Neither was conceding an inch. An attractive girl sat on the bar in a long nightdress playing *Sweet Violets* on a mouth organ. Several others, who must have wisely taken an early night, were standing around enjoying a 'heartstarter', the first beer of the day. Mick the fencer was asleep on a stool at the end of the bar. His dog also lay asleep under his stool.

Sunday morning had an entirely different quality from the rest of the meeting. The airstrip swarmed with activity as aircraft taxied and took off to their various destinations. As before, some revellers were still asleep under aircraft wings, slumbering somehow through the din of revving engines. Fine dust rose up and hung in the air as various vehicles pulled away. Yet a great many were reluctant to make a move. They stood around yarning and drinking, ankle deep in discarded cans. Contact, companionship was being stretched out as long as possible; some visitors would not leave until midday Monday. Kevin came walking back from a farewell at the airstrip, barefoot at last; he had slung his plastic shoes away; nothing could tell us more emphatically that the carnival was over. Still, Kevin, too, was loath to make the final handshakes and depart.

But it had gone. Another race meeting was over. Birdsville would have another twelve months to get over it before the next one.

Mick the Simpson Desert fencer could sleep at peace at last.

4 CHANTILLY

Brough Scott

It is mid-morning in Paris on the first Sunday in June. Already the day is heavily hot under a milky blue sky, a day for shirtsleeves. A quick glance across the Place de Roubaix at the station clock in the Gare du Nord tells it is almost eleven. Just time for one last aperitif at the kerbside table. Then we rise and sidle into the steady, and swelling, stream of summer-clad people bustling into the station, along a crowded platform and into a waiting train.

They, and we, are on our way to the biggest racing event of the French summer, the Prix de Jockey Club (The French Derby) at Chantilly. It's the number two race on the French calendar – equivalent of the Caulfield Cup, the Preakness or the King George at Ascot. Only the Prix de l'Arc de Triomphe, in the smoky autumn mists of October, outranks it. But not in prize money. In 1975 the Chantilly classic was worth £147,000 – the richest stakes race in the world. Today we shall see an international field of brilliant three-year-olds gallop a mile and a half around a dipping U-shaped course in the old château town forty-two kilometres north of Paris. We shall need plenty of time to savour in full both the course and the character of the racing. That's why we leave Paris early.

Our train clicks swiftly northwards through the encroaching city streets that fade into factory-dominated industrial suburbs, then into open, flat country. After fifteen minutes of this the dark green of the Forêt de Chantilly sweeps forward to surround us. Less than forty minutes since the carriage doors banged shut at the Gare du Nord we are decanted at the bare, un-imposing station of Chantilly. (When racing began here in the 1830s, it took half a day to come up from Paris by coach. Nowadays Parisians are perhaps the world's most pampered racegoers. Except for a short winter break and a brief summer adjournment to Deauville, they have racing all year. All the tracks can be reached within an hour from the heart of Paris: Longchamp, on the southern tip of the Bois de Boulogne and St. Cloud just across the river from there; Maison Laffitte, in the city's eastern suburbs; new, ultra-modern Every, just ten minutes further along the autoroute du Sud from Orly Airport; and the two famous old jumping tracks of Enghein and Auteuil, both quite central.)

Jostled up and across the wooden footbridge spanning the railway tracks, we stumble into the tree-lined half-moon of the station square, alive with racegoers wriggling their way through rows of parked cars. We plop down at an outdoor table in front of the Cafe de la Gare. The garçon grimaces as we order an economy lunch: *lapin aux herbes* (rabbit stew), half a carafe of red wine, small wedge of camembert and coffee. Some economy: on Chantilly's biggest day of the year this slightly overgrown snack cost 50 francs (£6 or $11). Inside, the press of noisy people is heavy at the rear of the cafe. The establishment also serves as a tabac, one of 4,000 'betting shops' throughout France which handle off-course bets on the main race meeting of the day. Each Sunday millions of French men and women bet the Tierce, the one-two-three place forecast bet, which, since 1952, has become the national gambling passion (and pumps £30 million into the arteries of French racing each year. It has also been instrumental in nearly quadrupling the horse population of Chantilly in the twenty-five years from 1950, when it was only 950). We note some punters are flapping their franc notes at the Tierce agent with rising agitation: all bets must be placed by twelve o'clock and noon is almost upon us.

More people have poured off a newly-arrived train, bubbling waves of humanity that will build into a squashed and perspiring crowd of 100,000 later at the course. How different is this very square at six o'clock each weekday morning when famous trainers, bulky in anoraks above brown, dew-spangled wellingtons pad from their cars into the cafe for their post-workout coffee. At their elbows strut their jockeys, who are fashion-plate manikins, miniature dudes. Their hair is sleekly-coiffed, their faces sharp angles of tightly-drawn flesh. Their burgundy or biscuit-coloured skivvies rise to their throats from beneath high-life lambswool sweaters; their exquisitely-cut jodphurs with leather facings running inside each leg from knee to ankle seem to end in two peeps of sand-flecked riding boots. This is Horseman's Chic, by Vogue out of Harper's Bazaar.

The dawn chat across the tables is all horses; outsiders' ears stay pricked; attention rivets on the top trainers. The impassive Maurice Zilber, for instance, sitting quietly and fending off the queries of the hangers-on. Egyptian-born Zilber bankrolled himself into the trainer's game through punting, made his name winning big races for the 150-horse-strong Wildenstein stable, then achieved even greater successes for the American Nelson Bunker-Hunt, especially with champion filly Dahlia. Across the table is Zilber's great rival, Angel Penna. Before coming to France, Penna was top trainer in his native Argentina, then Venezuela and Miami. In 1972, his first year, San San won the Arc de Triomphe for him; he then joined Wildenstein and, ironically, raised the great filly Allez France into Dahlia's big rival. At this dawn gathering, you can also hear the assorted accents of the best trainers in France: the clipped cavalry tones of Francois Mathet, ten times French champion trainer; noted imports such as Van de Poele from Belgium, Millbank from England and Paus from Sweden. They, and Australian Scobie Breasley, have been lured here, or brought here, for money, big money. One example will suffice: in 1974 7,349 horses ran in France for £14,630,307 in prize money – an average of £1,990 per horse. The same year 6,560 horses in England pursued £4,962,208 – average per horse: £756. It is not surprising that these men, in garb and easy demeanour, ooze prosperity as they converse quietly, their voices lost beneath the crackle of people snapping open and folding their copies of their daily racing bible, *Le Sport Complet*.

Back at our lunchtime table we need that newspaper more than these informed insiders ever will. For those with shaky French, the long-established turf Franglais is a blessing – le favorite, le crack jockey, le outsider, etc. By the time we have struggled through the forecasts and ringed our selections, it is 1:15 and time to stroll the half mile to the course.

Along the way, we can occasionally glimpse through the trees a distant rooftop, a flash of window panes of the large, ordered houses you would expect to find in any chi-chi dormitory suburb less than an hour's commuter trainride from a nation's capital city. Many of the good solid burghers inside these houses are hard at work, chewing and sipping their way through the five-course meal and vintage wine list that are their raceday lunch. In an hour or so they will purr to the track in chauffeur-driven limousines. It is their day to be seen.

They avoid the crush of people. We don't, and it keeps building up ceaselessly. We bob along in the human tide flowing eastwards from the station across Route Nationale 16 from Paris. Once across, we are at the tree-lined perimeter of the racecouse itself. Stretching away in front and to the left is an open expanse of grassland, just large enough to contain the buckled 'U' shape of the track. From this vantage point we can see clearly what sets Chantilly apart from other racecourses. Two immense buildings. Both are magnificent. Beyond the course proper, at the bottom of the track's far turn, stands the moat-ringed Château de Chantilly. The Château consists of three parts: the Châtelet, built in 1560; the Grand Château where the Grand Condé and his descendants lives (it was destroyed in the Revolution and rebuilt in 1876–82); and the Château d'Enghien. J. H. Mansart, who, as chief architect for Louis XIV built the palace and chapel at Versailles, built the Grand Château here for the Prince de Condé, Louis XIV's cousin, and his finest general. The Great Condé himself was said to have laid out the gardens. He turned the Château into a meeting place for the savants and artists of the day. The Sun King, who admired the opulence of the Château attended a famous lavish banquet for 5,000 guests here in 1671. The following day, Condé's chef, Monsieur Vatel, killed himself: he had miscalculated the servings of the beef by two.

The Château was badly damaged in the Revolution. The Duc d'Aumale, who took it over after the last Condé died, had it restored (1876–82) then presented it and its superb art collection (Raphael, Poussin, Watteau and Clouet) to the Institut de France. Directly in front of the Château racegoers can see the Poste de Lions, the longest and most immaculately-prepared sand gallop in the world. Named after two stone lions who guard its entrance, it runs straight away from them for two and a half miles. Endless though it appears, the Poste de Lions is only a small stretch of the eighty-four hectares of sand and 116 of turf gallops laid down in the 6,000 acres of Chantilly forest (plus another forty kilometres of paths and tracks reserved for horses). Besides the training areas on the racecourse itself, there are five more near-by serving the seventy-five stables that are scattered throughout Chantilly and neighbouring villages of Lamorlaye, Coye la Forêt and Avilly St. Léonard. The complex is a profusion of leafy avenues that lead to stable yards, some of which are owned by luminaries like the Aga Khan, the Rothschilds, the Wertheimers, Boussac, Wildenstein and Volterra. Even in fabled Lexington, Kentucky, there is nothing to rival Chantilly for size and visual splendour.

Having drunk in the charms of the Grand Château, we pan our gaze well to the left to take in what appears to be another equally-imposing château. It is, in fact, Les Grandes Ecuries (The Big Stables), well named because these are by far the largest racing stables in the world. The Grand Condé's great grandson, the Duc d'Orléans, built the stables and housed there in palatial luxury some two hundred and forty horses and four hundred stag and boar hounds. The Duc d'Orléans and his great rival Lord Henry Seymour, dominated French Thoroughbred racing in the first half of the nineteenth century. The Duc's choosing of Englishman George Edwards as his trainer helped to establish the huge English racing colony at Chantilly, thought at one time to outnumber the French. By 1845, eleven years after Edwards arrived, Chantilly had twenty English trainers in charge of well over 200 horses. Down the years a steady number of small, bandy-legged men have shipped across the channel to settle into the training world of Chantilly. For almost 150 years, Chantilly has been one of the most tightly-knit English colonies in France.

Once Prime Minister to Louis XV, the Duc retired to Chantilly to indulge his passions: his mistresses, the arts, porcelain making and, especially, hunting. He ordered his peasants to hack the first riding paths through the thick, extensive forest. Today these rides, and others carved later, have become the world's most extensive sand gallops for the greatest concentration of Thoroughbred horseflesh in history. Here the horses and grounds are tended by more than sixty jockeys, three hundred associated traders, one thousand stable lads and another thousand assorted maintenance staff. The complex boasts a seventy-one-bed hospital, a 280-desk apprentices' school and three other centres for lads and apprentices. In 1975 some 3,440 horses trained here, more than twice the number at England's Newmarket or at Belmont in the United States. If the Duc d'Orléans's obsessive premonition has come true, he may well be one of those battalions of Thoroughbreds. Legend has it he was convinced he would be reincarnated as a horse and that he built Les Grandes Ecuries, this glorious folly, to provide suitable dwelling for his new life as a high class oats muncher.

If the Duc is still waiting to assume equine form to gallop Chantilly he could be getting impatient. Racing began here in 1834 after a Russian nobleman, Prince Labanoff, a guest at the Château, admired the springiness of the turf. He organised an impromptu race among guests along the sweep of turf beyond the lake. The first Prix de Jockey Club was held here in 1836.

Now, anxious to see that race almost one hundred and fifty years later, we wrench our gaze from the Ecuries and thread our way to the right and into the course proper. For only eight francs (about one pound) we can enter and walk freely in any area except a small, railed-off enclosure in front of the weighing room; this is reserved for owners, trainers and racing connections. On this packed classic day it is a mercy the nabobs have not been granted larger breathing space. The course suffers a major flaw in layout; the entire 100,000 crowd has to compress itself into the two hundred yards wide strip running between the southern connecting road and the rails of the finishing straight. A jostling journey to see the parading horses in the paddock at the western end of the course will almost certainly mean missing the next race, perhaps two, from a decent vantage point. Punters wanting to bet also curse the *pari mutuel* betting monopoly. Clerks at the windows cannot handle bets fast enough. Gigantic queues develop. English and Australian punters actually find themselves yearning for their odds-paring adversaries, the bookmakers. At least you can transact instant business with them. More than any other French course Chantilly in the mid-1970s, sorely needed a computerised tote. (Its list of discomforts could one day cost it the Prix de Jockey Club.)

Still, the sights and ambiance compensate hugely for the problems in placing bets. Many of the women are stunning, displaying that matchless French talent for wearing simply-tailored and coordinated clothes with great elegance.

Whatever degree of chic the best-turned-out ladies achieve, they really cannot match the ravishing spectacle of the best stretches of the racing. After a Gallicly-melodramatic walk then return canter in front of the stands, the horses move to the starting stalls to ready themselves for the clockwise gallop. They're off and their progress along the back straight is an unforgettable spectacle: a vivid harlequin patch of bright jockey's silks rippling past Les Grandes Ecuries. A short distance further on, they peel around the sharp right-hand turn and the glistening horses, with bright dabs of colour above them, seem to skitter across the face of the Château. The blending of moving and still images is brief; the horses are now around the final turn and pounding to the finishing line.

Who won? The winner's name is boomed out, hissed Gallic exclamations rise up; torn remnants of *tierce* tickets flutter down to the ground in thousands of tiny blue snowstorms. Today's winner of the Prix goes into the almanacs; he has gained a sliver of immortality. Lasting forever. It seems to fit Chantilly. Both the Château and Les Grandes Ecuries look as if they will grace the background as long as that. You hope so, because the Ecuries are surely the most coruscating backdrop you will ever see from a racecourse grandstand. They bestow grandeur, making every horse that streams past appear a noble specimen of the breed.

When the meeting is over, we are pummelled along in the churning crowd, through the gates and up to the main road. The café in the square and the trains will be packed. Let the mob disperse. We'll cross Route Nationale 16 to look over Les Aigles, the tree-lined sand gallops with a central turf area on which Napoleon was said to have trained his legions. Gazing along them you wish the Duc d'Orléans's dream had come true; that he had at some time come back maned and four-footed to pound along these lovely gallops. He loved the horse; and the horse emphatically reigns here. The Duc's spirit must still be out there somewhere.

5 THE WHITE TURF
Unconventional horse racing in Switzerland

John Sheppard

'The White Turf' is the intriguing title given to horse racing on a frozen lake covered with a smoothed and perfectly level layer of snow. The sport embraces flat racing, steeplechasing, harness racing (trotting) and skijöring, in which galloping horses each tow a single skier. *Concours Hippique*, or show jumping, is also part of it.

Apart from skijöring, which comes from Norway, the white turf is a fusion of men, horses and snow as distinctively Swiss as fondue cookery and numbered bank accounts, but much rarer than either. Whereas you can wield a fondue fork in Melbourne or Montevideo, or slide your money quietly out of sight in Bermuda or the Cayman Islands rather than in Zürich, there are only two places where you can see the white turf in its true form. They are at St Moritz and Arosa, which are among the most chic and popular winter resorts in Europe. Both perch at high altitudes (St Moritz 6,089 feet above sea level; Arosa 5,904) in The Grisons, a canton sitting astride the Alps in Switzerland's south-east corner, its 2,800 square miles making it the largest of the twenty-two Swiss cantons.

The white turf season is very brief; blink slowly and you miss it. Between them the two resorts hold no more than six meetings each mid-winter, in January and February. With daylight scarce, the racecard at each track has to be short: five races, compared to seven or eight at conventional meetings elsewhere. The final race on any programme starts at four o'clock, when the rushing horses pursue or tow their own purplish, daddy-longlegs shadows across a white sward dimpled with the dark hollows of hoofprints.

At Arosa, which, from the mid-1960s, displaced St Moritz as Switzerland's dressiest and most formal winter resort, they stage just two forms of racing – flat galloping and steeplechase. St Moritz, on the other hand, serves a mixed salad, its usual racecard offering two galloping races, a trotting race, a skijöring dash and finally a steeplechase. As well as its race meetings, St Moritz

holds an annual *Concours Hippique* in late January. It has become the surviving venue for the sport on snow in Switzerland, a contraction we shall look at later in more detail.

For that small band of racegoers who consider racing first and only as an aesthetic spectacle, this scarcity of white turf meetings is a sadness; for this is perhaps the most visually beguiling form of horseracing. To begin with, the settings at St Moritz and Arosa are majestic. At both places the horses perform against a distant backcloth comprising an immense sweep of Alpine peaks streaked with dark green fir forests on their lower slopes and thrusting upwards thousands of feet in tucks and folds of glistening white.

On most race days, an observer's gaze continuing upwards beyond the jagged horizon, swims into a sky of sparkling azure, a sky so intensely blue it startles first-time visitors. Reflecting the glare from the snow, the winter light in The Grisons has been described as 'pitilessly brilliant'; tinted sun glasses are a must. The dry, rarified air ('ethereal champagne' to one nineteenth-century visitor) produce an abundance of winter sunshine along the wide, sixty-miles long Engadine Valley, where St Moritz is situated, and throughout the upper Schanffig basin to the north-east, where Arosa is located. In fact, St Moritz was launched and became pre-eminent among Swiss winter resorts – and a home for snow racing – because the sun shines there so often during the winter.

In the autumn of 1864, Johannes Badrutt, the legendary owner of the Kulm Hotel, invited a group of visiting Englishmen to return and spend the entire following winter at the Kulm free of charge. If they did not find it warmer and sunnier than London from January through April, he would pay all their travelling expenses from London to St Moritz and return. They arrived swaddled to the eyebrows, perspiring profusely with their unguarded eyes half-blinded by the sun's glare. Badrutt, who greeted them on the steps of his hotel in shirtsleeves, predicted accurately that his money was safe. Thus began the English love affair with St Moritz (for more than a century they have always been the most frequent visitors) and later a multitude of other Swiss resorts. The perennial presence of the English, whose passion for racing does not have to be dwelt upon, helps to explain why the resort includes the white turf among its unexcelled list of winter attractions. Arosa, too, is much favoured by visitors with Union Jacks on their luggage tags.

So, dazzling sunshine is almost certainly present to enhance high-quality racing that is rich with sights and atmosphere unlike any the most experienced racegoers will have seen and felt at conventional tracks. Each race, especially the gallops, is a mobile painting: the sheen of thoroughbred horseflesh; plumes of frosted breath spurting form the horses' mouths and nostrils; the pointillist clusters of jockeys' colours brilliantly vivid above the whiteness; the diamond glitter of sunflashes on tinted goggles. Silent explosions of snow burst up from the horses' softly-drumming hooves; rooster

For snow trotting races on their frozen lake, St Moritz authorities provide sulkies set much higher than the wheeled variety.

tails of snow spray back from the runners of trotting sledges, all catching and refracting sunlight into shimmering bands of rainbow colour. The entire field of horses is in clear view from start to finish: no fog, foliage or dips in the terrain blot out a single stride of the action. In bad weather, when a snowfall does cut back visibility, the running horses and riders, seen blurred through the snow curtain and eerily silent, have a kind of surrealist charm.

As the look and muted sound of the white turf are different, so too are the crowds and ambiance; they are not remotely duplicated on racecourses elsewhere. To note the differences, come along to the Pferderennen (horse-racing) at St Moritz on the more important of its two racedays. On this programme the main race, usually with 19–20 starters, is the Grosser Preis von St Moritz, offering prize money of 25,000 francs (£5,680), well above the average rewards on English tracks. The long oval of the track itself has been marked in the snow on Lake St Moritz, the only features rising above ground level on the course proper being the running rails and finishing post. The lake lies between the resort's two parts – St Moritz Dorf, spread on a mountain terrace two hundred feet above the lake, and the ancient spa of St Moritz Bad in the plain south of it.

Thousands of people have turned up. Most are tourists because they far outnumber the local burghers; the meeting is staged for their recreation and the Swiss themselves are not wildly ardent followers of horseracing – at any time of year their sporting pursuits are active rather than passive. Dozens of gleaming cars parked in very precise rows next to the saddling enclosure proclaim that many visitors have motored from nearby villages: Chamfer, Silvaplana, Samedan and the famous mountaineering resort of Ponteresina.

Most of the racegoers needed no transport at all to get here. Tourists based at St Moritz, and residents, have simply ambled down the slopes from their hotels, houses and chalets. It is perfect for the languid or disorganised. You can be gulping your last cup of lunchtime coffee in the hotel dining room when the horses are parading for the first race and be down at the rail – perhaps breathing a little hard – for the Off. Or, if you are staying in a room or suite on a side of one of several de luxe hotels – the Schweizerhof, Steffani's, the Engadiner Kulm, the Carlton – that overlooks the lake, you can watch from bedroom or balcony with a whisky and soda at your elbow. Royal Ascot, Belmont Park and Flemington, for all their splendours and amenities, are hell-holes compared with convenience on this order.

An observer circulating widely will notice unusual features of both the composition and attire of the crowd. There seem to be a great many children, playing and chattering among themselves, draped over the railings of the saddling enclosure or standing politely silent in one of the many totalisator (*pari mutuel*) queues while mama and papa frown and chew pencils over their form sheets. When a racecourse is open and an integral part of a

Thoroughbreds gallop confidently along the snow-covered lake at St Moritz: it is the smoothest and most even surface on which horse-racing is held.

holiday township's topography, racegoing develops naturally and easily into a family affair. It does help, too, for tolerance of children that there are no raucously bellowing bookmakers present.

As you would expect at a winter resort, the clothing has a uniformity that seems decidedly odd at a race meeting. You just can't recognise who's who. No suits of gaudy check pattern identify the Runyonesque horseplayers; no grey toppers and cutaway coats mark men of distinction; no bullet-proof tweeds of the Evelyn Waugh mode proclaim the horse-mad squirocracy though some are doubtless present; no thousand-guinea Yves St Laurent originals or Hartnell chapeaux classify the moneyed elite from the off-the-rack proletariat. A local delicatessen owner or telephone switchgirl, a holidaying accountant and his wife from St Albans (or Frankfurt) look much the same in this crowd as such noted winter visitors as Herbert von Karajan, Lord Fraser (of the House of Fraser, which owns Harrods), Christina Onassis, Princess Ira von Furstenberg or the Prince of Lichtenstine. Everybody is buttoned and wrapped against the sharp cold in a near-

standard turnout of fur hat or skicap, sunglasses, bulky topcoat or sheepskin jacket, gloves or mittens, ski-trousers and snowboots. From the distance you can't discern whether an ensemble set back its wearer a total of £100 ($180) of £2,000 ($3,600). Nor is a deep, deep suntan the sign of a leisured money-bags, because everybody has one. The natty fellow of mahogany brown watching the runners parade under their richly-coloured horseblankets could be an international playboy just arrived from Monte Carlo, or merely Karl, the village postman. A white turf meeting must be a maddening experience for pickpockets.

What this homogenized and friendly crowd of people have come to see is horseracing that is very young compared to its original green turf versions in England and France. The various types of snow racing all came late to St Moritz, well after its counter attractions of skiing, tobogganing, skating, curling, bandy (a Celtic form of icehockey) and the Cresta Run. Old records suggest it began with laissez-faire skijöring on the frozen lake in the early 1890s. Horses were recruited from merchants, deliverymen and nearby farmers. Among the pioneer skijörers (perhaps surprising in a chauvanistic country where most women did not get the vote until the 1960s) were women, whose long dresses flapped and billowed around them – skisuits with the sprayed-on look were far into the future. After this pipeopener variations of skijöring were brought in . . . and seemingly discarded. For instance, in 1895 St Moritz also offered a horseless version of skijöring called 'husbands in harness'. A lovely photograph shows a line of men in jackets and knickerbockers skating furiously over the lake, each man holding in his right hand the leading end of a thick rope or a straight sapling – the towline. The skaters are straining from the exertions of towing their long-skirted, sun-bonneted wives, who are bending forward primly from the waist on their skis to grasp the towlines two-handed. The shoreline is black with rows of people standing quiet and sedate as if wondering what to make of it all.

This must have been a passing fancy: in 1906, when five lively Norwegians organized the first official skijöring race on the lake only horses were called upon to do the hauling. For some reason, conditions at the lake were un-suitable so the organisers had to turn the event into a cross-country race. Horses and skiers were mustered at the Post-Plaz in St Moritz Dorf. In gloomy and bitingly cold weather, they sped down the Bahnhofstrasse, through corridors of spectators four or five deep. Then they swept along a wriggling course around the lake's edge, through St Moritz Bad to Chamfer and back to Steffani's Hotel. During the race, a number of unwary strollers had to leap from the path of the galloping horses. Despite these perils, the race was a great success, the harbinger of what developed into the white turf programmes of today.

The following year (1907) the first trotting races were held on the lake and, in 1908, galloping races; after this skijöring came formally onto the

Unseasonable spell at Royal Ascot? No, this is a skijöring race at Gstaad, winter home of many moneyed, or merely famous, people.

In early skijöring races at St Moritz, local farm horses pulled the skiers. When thoroughbreds were introduced, some found the business of towing a skier distracting.

racecards. When thoroughbreds were first introduced to skijöring, many of them were unhappy at pulling the skier, who was far behind and sometimes veered from a line directly to the horse's rear; the horses seemed to prefer the man with the reins in his accustomed position – on their backs. Before skijöring came off the snowy streets it had become a hazard for both pedestrians and skijörers. The *Engadine Year Book* of 1909 announced: 'Owing to the numerous complaints received by the police of driverless horses being encountered on the public roads, it was held desirable to impose a 'test' on members before they were allotted horses for use on the highways. Furthermore, the authorities issued a notice to all livery stable keepers forbidding them to let out horses to people who did not possess the licence issued by the St Moritz Skijöring Club'.

Shortly after World War I snow racing began at Arosa which, like St Moritz, had for centuries been a noted spa. Here, too, race fields quickly became international and of high quality.

For many years all the horses wore normal horseshoes. The style changed after a Munich horseowner shod his trotters with a special shoe to which he had forged extra toe and hoof patches to give the horses better purchase. Riders who know both types say snow feels underhoof like a heavy sand track, although the snow, which does not cohere to the same degree, spurts much more than damp sand.

Two of the main types of racing surface, sand and cinders (which are commonly used throughout the United States), pack down into a substantially harder consistency than snow. This means that on the firmer sand horses achieve greater thrust with their legs and can therefore run faster. With their hooves sinking that little further into snow, galloping horses and trotters use about a third more energy than they do on sand, cinders or grass. To allow for this, owners bringing their charges onto snow compute the extra drain on energy before entering them in longer races, run over 2,400 and 2,800 metres.

While the white turf is slower, it is the truest and safest of all racing surfaces; its base, the frozen lake, is perfectly flat and the covering layer of snow is assiduously combed free of all undulations before each race meeting. Feeling such a level and reliable footing under them trotters are less likely to break their gait, as they often do on other surfaces; white turf punters appreciate this fact. Trotting drivers and horses new to the white turf need hard practice to adapt themselves to it. At St Moritz, the Racing Association supplies specially-built racing sledges. These weigh the same as conventional harness racing sulkies but are designed to raise the driver much higher to prevent his being drenched, or perhaps blinded, in snow sprays from the sledge runners and horses' hooves. To compete effectively, each driver must learn his new perspectives and his horse must get used to different centres of balance of both man and the vehicle he is pulling.

The other snow sport for horses, show jumping, was introduced long after the rest. In 1922 Gstaad, which lies at 3,543 feet at the junction of four gently-sloping valleys in the Bernese Oberland, put on its first *Concours Hippique*. Many of the best Swiss riders competed. There was a sputter of random horse shows at other winter resorts until, in 1951, Davos launched its annual *Concours* with fences set down on a natural ice rink covered with snow. Like white turf racing, it is a brilliant spectacle. Its flow of colours – vivid red jackets launching from white mass, passing in quick outline against sapphire-blue sky to drop back into white again – gives the snow version a splendour well above summer show jumping on grass and makes it a world apart from the semi-stygian gloom of indoor meetings, like those at the Wembley Pool in London. Down the years standards have been consistently high with luminaries such as British riders David Broome and Paddy McMahon competing in fields stiff with the best European talent. Swiss riders often fared well; their proud cavalry tradition makes this one of their major equine sports in summer. Above-the-line prize money was never the lure for the best riders: even as late as 1975 in St Moritz the fattest first prize for a declared professional was only 250 francs (£50/$100).

Sadly these wonderfully attractive show jumping competitions proved perishable, except at St Moritz. In the mid-1960s, Gstaad stopped its annual show. The most scenic and fashionable resort in a canton considered Europe's most remarkable natural holiday area, Gstaad had too many fine rival things to offer: icehockey, ski-meetings, curling, tobogganing and a multitude of scintillating ski runs for personal sport. Its noted winter residents (who include Princess Grace and the Aga Khan) and lesser mortals preferred the challenge of piste and ice rink to the gentler pleasure of show jumping. In 1975, the pincer movement of inflation and dwindling attendances finally crushed the Davos show jumping as well. Six years earlier, 1969, just under 3,500 spectators had attended, permitting the organizers to make a splendid seventy-three francs profit on a turnover of F79,155. Four inflation-ravaged years later, only 2,235 people came along and the show ran F34,117 into the red. Only two more took place.

The white turf has been, and will remain a sliver of horse racing that most people will never have a chance to see at first hand. On the longest list of race classics its apogee, the Grosser Preis von St Moritz, would not rate a mention, even as a footnote. This doesn't matter a lot because a more coruscating setting in which to absorb the most fundamental pleasure of racing – the rippling grace and power of thoroughbred horses at full stretch – has yet to be discovered.

6 NEVER KNEW SUCH A FELLOW FOR 'OSSES

James Herriot

Probably the most dramatic occurrence in the history of veterinary practice was the disappearance of the draught horse. It is an almost incredible fact that this glory and mainstay of the profession just melted quietly away within a few years. And I was one of those who were there to see it happen.

When I first came to Darrowby the tractor had already begun to take over, but tradition dies hard in the agricultural world and there were still a lot of horses around. Which was just as well because my veterinary education had been geared to things equine with everything else a poor second. It had been a good scientific education in many respects but at times I wondered if the people who designed it still had a mental picture of the horse doctor with his top hat and frock coat busying himself in a world of horse-drawn trams and brewers' drays.

We learned the anatomy of the horse in great detail, then that of the other animals much more superficially. It was the same with the other subjects; from animal husbandry with such insistence on a thorough knowledge of shoeing that we developed into amateur blacksmiths – right up to medicine and surgery where it was much more important to know about glanders and strangles than canine distemper. Even as we were learning, we youngsters knew it was ridiculous, with the draught horse already cast as a museum piece and the obvious potential of cattle and small animal work.

Still, after we had absorbed a vast store of equine lore it was a certain comfort that there were still a lot of patients on which we could try it out. I should think in my first two years I treated farm horses nearly every day and though I never was and never will be an equine expert there was a strange thrill in meeting with the age-old conditions whose names rang down almost from medieval times. Quittor, fistulous withers, poll evil, thrush, shoulder slip – vets had been wrestling with them for hundreds of years using very much the same drugs and procedures as myself. Armed

The world's most famous vet, James Herriot, with friend.

51

with my firing iron and box of blister, I plunged determinedly into what had always been the surging mainstream of veterinary life.

And now, in less than three years the stream had dwindled, not exactly to a trickle but certainly to the stage where the final dry-up was in sight. This meant, in a way, a lessening of the pressures on the veterinary surgeon because there is no doubt that horse work was the roughest and most arduous part of our life.

So that today, as I looked at the three-year-old gelding, it occurred to me that this sort of thing wasn't happening as often as it did. He had a long tear in his flank where he had caught himself on barbed wire and it gaped open whenever he moved. There was no getting away from the fact that it had to be stitched.

The horse was tied by the head in his stall, his right side against the tall wooden partition. One of the farm men, a hefty six footer, took a tight hold of the head collar and leaned back against the manger as I puffed some iodoform into the wound. The horse didn't seem to mind, which was a comfort because he was a massive animal emanating an almost tangible vitality and power. I threaded my needle with a length of silk, lifted one of the lips of the wound and passed it through. This was going to be no trouble, I thought, as I lifted the flap at the other side and pierced it, but as I was drawing the needle through, the gelding made a convulsive leap and I felt as though a great wind had whistled across the front of my body. Then, strangely, he was standing there against the wooden boards as if nothing had happened.

Portrait of an odd couple: the business end of a mean-tempered horse and the remains of a slow-moving veterinary surgeon.

52

On other occasions when I have been kicked I have never seen it coming. It is surprising how quickly those great muscular legs can whip out. But there was no doubt he had had a good go at me because my needle and silk was nowhere to be seen, the big man at the head was staring at me with wide eyes in a chalk white face and the front of my clothing was in an extraordinary state. I was wearing a gaberdine mac and it looked as if somebody had taken a razor blade and painstakingly cut the material into narrow strips which hung down in ragged strips to ground level. The great iron-shod hoof had missed my legs by an inch or two but my mac was a write-off.

I was standing there looking around me in a kind of stupor when I heard a cheerful hail from the doorway.

'Now then, Mr Herriot, what's he done at you?' Cliff Tyreman, the old horseman, looked me up and down with a mixture of amusement and asperity.

'He's nearly put me in hospital, Cliff,' I replied shakily. 'About the closest near miss I've ever had. I just felt the wind of it.'

'What were you tryin' to do?'

'Stitch that wound, but I'm not going to try any more. I'm off to the surgery to get a chloroform muzzle.'

The little man looked shocked. 'You don't need no chloroform. I'll haud him and you'll have no trouble.'

'I'm sorry, Cliff.' I began to put away my suture materials, scissors and powder. 'You're a good bloke, I know, but he's had one go at me and he's not getting another chance. I don't want to be lame for the rest of my life.'

The horseman's small, wiry frame seemed to bunch into a ball of aggression. He thrust forward his head in a characteristic posture and glared at me. 'I've never heard owt as daft in me life.' Then he swung round on the big man who was still hanging on to the horse's head, the ghastly pallor of his face now tinged with a delicate green. 'Come on out o' there, Bob! You're that bloody scared you're upsetting t'oss. Come on out of it and let me have 'im!'

Bob gratefully left the head and, grinning sheepishly, moved with care along the side of the horse. He passed Cliff on the way and the little man's head didn't reach his shoulder.

Cliff seemed thoroughly insulted by the whole business. He took hold of the head collar and regarded the big animal with the disapproving stare of a headmaster at a naughty child. The horse, still in the mood for trouble, laid back his ears and began to plunge about the stall, his huge feet clattering ominously on the stone floor, but he came to rest quickly as the little man uppercutted him furiously in the ribs.

'Get stood up straight there, ye big bugger. What's the matter with ye?' Cliff barked and again he planted his tiny fist against the swelling barrel

of the chest, a puny blow which the animal could scarcely have felt but which reduced him to quivering submission. 'Try to kick, would you, eh? I'll bloody fettle you!' He shook the head collar and fixed the horse with a hypnotic stare as he spoke. Then he turned to me. 'You can come and do your job, Mr Herriot, he won't hurt tha.'

I looked irresolutely at the huge, lethal animal. Stepping open-eyed into dangerous situations is something vets are called upon regularly to do and I suppose we all react differently. I know there were times when an over-vivid imagination made me acutely aware of the dire possibilities and now my mind seemed to be dwelling voluptuously on the frightful power in those enormous shining quarters, on the unyielding flintiness of the spatulate feet with their rims of metal. Cliff's voice cut into my musings.

'Come on, Mr Herriot, I tell ye he won't hurt tha.'

I reopened my box and tremblingly threaded another needle. I didn't seem to have much option; the little man wasn't asking me, he was telling me. I'd have to try again.

I couldn't have been a more impressive sight as I shuffled forwards, almost tripping over the tattered hula-hula skirt which dangled in front of me, my shaking hands reaching out once more for the wound, my heart thundering in my ears. But I needn't have worried. It was just as the little man had said; he didn't hurt me. In fact he never moved. He seemed to be listening attentively to the muttering which Cliff was directing into his face from a few inches' range. I powdered and stitched and clipped as though working on

Cliff, the old groom, had nothing against modern medicines, but thought the finest remedy to quiet a jumpy horse was a 'bunch of fives' to the ribs.

54

an anatomical specimen. Chloroform couldn't have done it any better.

As I retreated thankfully from the stall and began again to put away my instruments the monologue at the horse's head began to change its character. The menacing growl was replaced by a wheedling, teasing chuckle.

'Well, ye see, you're just a daft awd bugger, getting yourself all airigated over nowt. You're a good lad, really, aren't ye, a real good lad.' Cliff's hand ran caressingly over the neck and the towering animal began to nuzzle his cheek, as completely in his sway as any Labrador puppy.

When he had finished he came slowly from the stall, stroking the back, ribs, belly and quarters, even giving a playful tweak at the tail on parting, while what had been a few minutes ago an explosive mountain of bone and muscle submitted happily.

I pulled a packet of Gold Flake from my pocket. 'Cliff, you're a marvel. Will you have a cigarette?'

'It 'ud be like giving a pig a strawberry,' the little man replied, then he thrust forth his tongue on which reposed a half-chewed gobbet of tobacco. 'It's allus there. Ah push it in fust thing every mornin' soon as I get out of bed and there it stays. You'd never know, would you?'

I must have looked comically surprised because the dark eyes gleamed and the rugged little face split into a delightful grin. I looked at that grin – boyish, invincible – and reflected on the phenomenon that was Cliff Tyreman.

In a community in which toughness and durability was the norm he stood out as something exceptional. When I had first seen him nearly three years ago barging among cattle, grabbing their noses and hanging on effortlessly, I had put him down as an unusually fit middle-aged man; but he was in fact nearly seventy. There wasn't much of him but he was formidable; with his long arms swinging, his stumping, pigeon-toed gait and his lowered head he seemed always to be butting his way through life.

'I didn't expect to see you today,' I said. 'I heard you had pneumonia.'

He shrugged. 'Aye, summat of t'sort. First time I've ever been off work since I was a lad.'

'And you should be in your bed now, I should say.' I looked at the heaving chest and partly open mouth. 'I could hear you wheezing away when you were at the horse's head.'

'Nay, I can't stick that nohow. I'll be right in a day or two.' He seized a shovel and began busily clearing away the heap of manure behind the horse, his breathing loud and stertorous in the silence.

Harland Grange was a large, mainly arable farm in the low country at the foot of the Dale, and there had been a time when this stable had had a horse standing in every one of the long row of stalls. There had been over twenty with at least twelve regularly at work, but now there were only two, the young horse I had been treating and an ancient grey called Badger.

Cliff had been head horseman and when the revolution came he turned to tractoring and other jobs around the farm with no fuss at all. This was typical of the reaction of thousands of other farm workers throughout the country; they didn't set up a howl at having to abandon the skills of a life-time and start anew – they just got on with it. In fact, the younger men seized avidly upon the new machines and proved themselves natural mechanics.

But to the old experts like Cliff, something had gone. He would say: 'It's a bloody sight easier sitting on a tractor – it used to play 'ell with me feet walking up and down them fields all day.' But he couldn't lose his love of horses; the fellow feeling between working man and working beast which had grown in him since childhood and was in his blood forever.

My next visit to the farm was to see a fat bullock with a piece of turnip stuck in his throat but while I was there, the farmer, Mr Gilling, asked me to have a look at old Badger.

'He's had a bit of a cough lately. Maybe it's just his age, but see what you think.'

The old horse was the sole occupant of the stable now. 'I've sold the three-year-old,' Mr Gilling said. 'But I'll still keep the old 'un – he'll be useful for a bit of light carting.'

I glanced sideways at the farmer's granite features. He looked the least sentimental of men but I knew why he was keeping the old horse. It was for Cliff.

'Cliff will be pleased anyway,' I said.

Mr Gilling nodded. 'Aye, I never knew such a feller for 'osses. He was never happier than when he was with them.' He gave a short laugh. 'Do you know, I can remember years ago when he used to fall out with his missus he'd come down to this stable of a night and sit among his 'osses. Just sit there for hours on end looking at 'em and smoking.'

7 WHITE HUNTER, RED FOX

Art Buchwald

Not long after my baptism of beagling, Mr John Huston, the movie director, who lives the life of Riley in Ireland between pictures, invited me to join him at his country estate one weekend to ride the hounds and hunt the foxes with the landed gentry of County Kildare.

When I arrived, Mr Huston gave the butler my bags and took me into the library. 'Now sit down, kid, I want to talk to you'.

'Yes sir, Mr Huston.'

'Now, kid, what exactly do you know about fox hunting?'

'Well, I've been reading up on it and Oscar Wilde said that fox hunting is the pursuit of the inedible by the unspeakable.'

Mr Huston blanched. 'That's just what I was afraid of. As long as you're going to be with us I think we'd better get you straight on fox hunting. Once you understand it, you'll realise what a wonderful thing fox hunting really is.'

'Yes, sir.'

'Fox hunting is one of the greatest and roughest sports in the world,' Mr Huston said. 'It is the real test of horsemanship, sportsmanship and woodmanship. And Irish fox hunting is the best fox hunting of all.'

'Why don't they just shoot the foxes and be done with it?' I asked.

'Because, kid, the only time you can shoot a fox is at night, and nine chances out of ten the farmer will only wound him and he will die a cruel, lingering death. In fox hunting, once the fox is trapped, he is entitled to a quick, clean death.'

'Why don't they gas them? That would do it.'

'You're missing the point. The fox serves a great purpose. The Irish people don't want to kill all the foxes. The fox is Ireland's best friend. If it weren't for the fox, there would be no great breed of Irish horses, those big-boned, heavy-muscled, bold, noble creatures who are responsible for the great steeplechase races throughout the world.

'And by the same token the fox is responsible for producing the great courage in Irish people. My boy, you haven't lived until you've seen an Irish woman, sixty-five or seventy years old, sitting side-saddle on a horse and taking one of the great Irish banks. The Irish love their fox hunting so much that every year a half-dozen oldsters fall out of their saddles and are dead before they hit the ground. They literally die with their boots on.

'And, oh, the women! The world owes a debt to the Irish women and to fox hunting. The Irish women are the mothers of Ireland's greatest export – Irishmen. I would go so far as to say that Guinness Stout and fox hunting are responsible for most of the good characteristics in Irishmen.'

'What is responsible for the bad ones?' I asked.

'Irish whiskey. But don't change the subject. Not only is fox hunting a humane sport, but it gives the fox a chance to get away. A fox is caught only one out of four times. Now what could be fairer?'

'Maybe if they imported a fox blight of some sort it would kill them off in no time,' I said.

'People say,' said Mr Huston, 'that fox hunting is a posh sport only for toffs, but I would say it was one of the most democratic sports there is. Anyone who can ride a horse is welcome to join in a fox hunt. This isn't just true of Ireland, it's true everywhere.'

Art Buchwald's notion of 'appropriate dress' did not quite coincide with the members' at an Irish hunt.

I disagreed. 'I had an uncle in Brooklyn who tried to join a fox hunt on Long Island, and the people set the hounds on him. Chased him all the way back to Brooklyn.'

Mr Huston was becoming annoyed. 'Look, kid, once you're out in the field on a horse you'll feel differently about this. I am going to take you on a fox hunt tomorrow and you'll see for yourself. Now, are there any more questions?'

'Well, there is one. Why don't they set out poison? It seems that would really knock them off.'

For the first time Mr Huston looked as if he was sorry he had asked me to come along.

The following morning was a 'grand, soft day', which means in Ireland that it was raining like hell. Originally, I had planned to wear a cowboy suit with two .45-calibre revolvers around my waist. But when the master of the hunt saw this he made me go back and change. I was given instead a pink, swallow-tailed coat, yellow vest, white tie, black boots and a tall silk hat. They wouldn't even let me keep my revolvers.

The horse Mr Huston had selected for me was a large, grey stallion named Lots of Lolly, a raring beast no different from any other jumping horse except that it talked a blue streak. Now there are people who say horses don't talk and it's true in most of the world. But Ireland, a country haunted by ghosts, inhabited by leprechauns and driven mad by banshees, is the exception. Horses not only talk here; you can't keep them quiet.

'You ever been fox hunting before?' Lots of Lolly asked.

'No, sir,' I honestly replied.

'I thought so,' he said. 'You really haven't a very good seat. Well, if you're game, I guess I am. But try to behave yourself. Don't pull on my mouth, and throw that damned whip away. Just leave everything to me.'

We had some time to wait before the hunt began and Lots of Lolly seemed very bored. 'Say, did ya hear the one about . . .'

'Hounds, gentlemen, please,' the master of the hunt said, and the whipper-ins, with the hounds neatly packed together, moved down to the first covert.

'What are they doing now?' I asked Lots of Lolly.

'Just wait. There, now the fox is going away, the hounds have the scent and they're giving tongue. Now the master is blowing "Gone Away" on his horn and the hunt is on. Let's go.'

I started off with Lots of Lolly trying to take the lead. The master of the hunt's face became contorted. 'If you please, sir, would you mind staying in the field?'

'Don't let him talk to you like that,' Lots of Lolly said. 'Are we hunting or are we not hunting? He's just a big bag of kale.' I was just about to tell the master of the hunt he was a bag of kale when the first bank loomed up in front of us.

'Close your eyes,' Lots of Lolly said, 'let go of the reins and leave everything to me.'

I closed my eyes but couldn't help peeping. When I saw what was in front of me I shrieked. Lots of Lolly became furious. 'I told you to shut your eyes – or would you prefer that I shut them for you?'

I shut them and Lots of Lolly soared beautifully over the bank, landing on all fours on the other side of the ditch.

'You see?' he said. 'What did I tell you? Now let's hear the music of the hounds.'

We turned and headed for the woods. Lots of Lolly was running three strides ahead of the rest of the hunt. Suddenly I looked ahead and saw a bank slightly higher than Mount Everest.

Lots of Lolly shuddered. 'Do you see what I see?'

'Yes, sir.'

'Are you willing to take a chance?'

'Yes, sir,' I said as we approached the jump.

'Well,' said Lots of Lolly, 'I'm not.'

And with that he stopped abruptly and threw me out of the saddle, over the bank into the water-filled ditch, and then, snickering with pleasure, galloped away.

Buchwald's mount, Lots of Lolly, inquires whether the humorist still finds riding to hounds a laughing matter.

Two hours later, while I was still swimming around in the mud, Lots of Lolly came back with the brush between his teeth.

'You certainly missed a wonderful hunt,' he said.

'What happened?'

'Well, we found a fox at Palmerstown which went to ground near the house. We went to Forenaughts, where we had a nice thirty minutes. At Tipperhaven, the hounds drew Ferness, where the fox left immediately and going for the kill he swung right-handed through Major Mainguy's bottoms leaving Arthurstown on his right. The hounds killed him in the open, just short of Kilteal Finish. And because I got there first they gave me the brush. You should have come along; you would have loved it.'

'Would you give me a ride back to town?' I asked him.

'With all that filthy goop on you? I should say not. What kind of horse do you think I am, anyhow?'

I told him, and Lots of Lolly went away mad.

8 THE GENUINE MEXICAN PLUG

Mark Twain

I resolved to have a horse to ride. I had never seen such wild, free, magnificent horsemanship outside of a circus as these picturesquely-clad Mexicans, Californians and Mexicanized Americans displayed in Carson streets every day. How they rode! Leaning just gently forward out of the perpendicular, easy and nonchalant, with broad slouch hat brim blown square up in front, and long *riata* swinging above the head, they swept through the town like the wind! The next minute they were only a sailing puff of dust on the far desert. If they trotted, they set up gallantly and gracefully, and seemed part of the horse; did not go jiggering up and down after the silly Miss-Nancy fashion of the riding-schools. I had quickly learned to tell a horse from a cow, and was full of anxiety to learn more. I was resolved to buy a horse.

While the thought was rankling in my mind, the auctioneer came scurrying through the plaza on a black beast that has as many humps and corners on him as a dromedary, and was necessarily uncomely; but he was 'going, going, at twenty-two! – horse, saddle and bridle at twenty-two dollars, gentleman!' and I could hardly resist.

A man whom I did not know (he turned out to be the auctioneer's brother) noticed the wistful look in my eye, and observed that that was a very remarkable horse to be going at such a price; and added that the saddle alone was worth the money. It was a Spanish saddle, with ponderous *tapidaros*, and furnished with the ungainly sole-leather covering with the unspellable name. I said I had half a notion to bid. Then this keen-eyed person appeared to me to be 'taking my measure'; but I dismissed the suspicion when he spoke, for his manner was full of guileless candour and truthfulness. Said he:

'I know that horse – know him well. You are a stranger, I take it, and so you might think he was an American horse, maybe, but I assure you he is not. He is nothing of the kind; but – excuse my speaking in a low voice, other people being near – he is, without the shadow of a doubt, a Genuine Mexican Plug!'

I did not know what a Genuine Mexican Plug was, but there was something about this man's way of saying it, that made me swear inwardly that I would own a Genuine Mexican Plug, or die.

'Has he any other-er-advantages?' I inquired, suppressing what eagerness I could.

He hooked his forefinger in the pocket of my army-shirt, led me to one side, and breathed in my ear impressively these words:

'He can out-buck anything in America!'

'Going, going, going – at twen-ty four dollars and a half, gen–'

'Twenty-seven!' I shouted, in a frenzy.

'And sold!' said the auctioneer, and passed over the Genuine Mexican Plug to me.

I could scarcely contain my exultation. I paid the money, and put the animal in a neighbouring livery-stable to dine and rest himself.

In the afternoon I brought the creature into the plaza, and certain citizens held him by the head, and others by the tail, while I mounted him. As soon as they let go, he placed all his feet in a bunch together, lowered his back, and then suddenly arched it upward, and shot me straight into the air a matter of three or four feet. I came as straight down again, lit in the saddle, went up instantly again, and came down on the horse's neck – all in the space of three or four seconds. Then he rose and stood almost straight up on his hind feet, and I, clasping his lean neck desperately, slid back into the saddle, and held on. He came down, and immediately hoisted his heels into the air, delivering a vicious kick at the sky, and stood on his forefeet. And then down he came once more, and began the original exercise of shooting me straight up again. The third time I went up I heard a stranger say:

'Oh, don't he buck, though.'

While I was up, somebody struck the horse a sounding thwack with a leathern strap, and when I arrived again the Genuine Mexican Plug was not there. A Californian youth chased him up and caught him, and asked if he might have a ride. I granted him that luxury. He mounted the Genuine, got lifted into the air once, but sent his spurs home as he descended, and the horse darted away like a telegram. He soared over three fences like a bird, and disappeared down the road toward the Washoe Valley.

I sat down on a stone, with a sigh, and by a natural impulse one of my hands sought my forehead, and the other the base of my stomach. I believe I never appreciated, till then, the poverty of the human machinery – for I still needed a hand or two to place elsewhere. Pen cannot describe how I was jolted up. Imagination cannot conceive how disjointed I was – how internally, externally and universally I was unsettled, mixed up and ruptured. There was a sympathetic crowd around me, though.

One elderly-looking comforter said:

'Stranger, you've been taken in. Everybody in this camp knows that horse. Any child, any Injun, could have told you that he'd buck; he is the very worst devil to buck on the continent of America. You *hear* me. I'm Curry. *Old* Curry. Old *Abe* Curry. And moreover he is a simon-pure, out-and-out, genuine d – – d Mexican Plug, and an uncommon mean one at that, too. Why, you turnip, if you had laid low and kept dark, there's chances to buy an American horse for mighty little more than you paid for that bloody old foreign relic.'

I gave no sign; but I made up my mind that if the auctioneer's brother's funeral took place while I was in the Territory I would postpone all other recreations to attend it.

After a gallop of sixteen miles the Californian youth and the Genuine Mexican Plug came tearing into town again, shedding foam flaked like spume-spray that drives before a typhoon, and, with one final skip over a wheelbarrow and a Chinaman, cast anchor in front of the 'ranch'.

Such panting and blowing! Such spreading and contracting of the red equine nostrils, and glaring of the wild equine eye! But was the imperial beast subjugated? Indeed he was not. His lordship the Speaker of the House thought he was, and mounted him to go down to the Capitol; but the first dash the creature made was over a pile of telegraph poles half as high as a church; and his time to the Capitol – one mile and three quarters – remains unbeaten to this day. But then he took an advantage – he left out the mile, and only did the three quarters. That is to say, he made a straight cut across lots, preferring fences and ditches to a crooked road; and when the Speaker got to the Capitol he said he had been in the air so much he held as if he had made the trip in a comet.

In the evening the Speaker came home afoot for exercise, and got the Genuine towed back behind a quartz wagon. The next day I loaned the animal to the Clerk of the House to go down to the Dana silver mine, six miles, and *he* walked back for exercise, and got the horse towed. Everybody I loaned him to always walked back; they never could get enough exercise any other way. Still, I continued to loan him to anybody who was willing to borrow him, my idea being to get him crippled, and throw him on the borrower's hands, or killed, and make the borrower pay for him.

But somehow nothing ever happened to him. He took chances that no other horse ever took and survived, but he always came out safe. It was his daily habit to try experiments that had always before been considered impossible, but he always got through. Sometimes he miscalculated a little, and did not get his rider through intact, but he *always* got through himself. Of course I had tried to sell him; but that was a stretch of simplicity which met with little sympathy. The auctioneer stormed up and down the streets on him for four days, dispersing the populace, interrupting business and destroying children and never got a bid – at least never any but the eighteen-dollar one he hired a notoriously substanceless bummer to make. The people only smiled pleasantly, and restrained their desire to buy, if they had any. Then the auctioneer brought in his bill, and I withdrew the horse from the market.

We tried to trade him off at private vendue next, offering him at a sacrifice for second-hand tombstones, old iron, temperance tracts – any kind of property. But holders were stiff, and we retired from the market again. I never tried to ride the horse any more. Walking was good enough exercise for a man like me, that had nothing the matter with him except ruptures, internal injuries, and such things. Finally I tried to *give* him away. But it was a failure. Parties said earthquakes were handy enough on the Pacific coast – they did not wish to own one. As a last resort I offered him to the Governor for use of the 'Brigade'. His face lit up eagerly at first, but toned down again, and he said the thing would not be palpable.

Just then the livery man brought in his bill for six weeks' keeping – stall-room for the horse, fifteen dollars; hay for the horse, two hundred and fifty! The Genuine Mexican Plug had eaten a ton of the article, and the man said he would have eaten a hundred if he had let him.

I will remark here, in all seriousness, that the regular price of hay during that year and a part of the next was really two hundred and fifty dollars a ton. During a part of the previous year it had sold at five hundred a ton, in gold, and during the winter before that there was such a scarcity of the article that in several instances small quantities had brought eight hundred dollars a ton in coin! The consequence might be guessed without my telling it: people turned their stock loose to starve, and before the spring arrived Carson and Eagle valleys were almost literally carpeted with their carcases. Any old settler there will verify these statements.

I managed to pay the livery bill, and that same day I gave the Genuine Mexican Plug to a passing Arkansas emigrant whom fortune delivered into my hand. If this ever meets his eye, he will doubtless remember the donation.

Now whoever has had the luck to ride a real Mexican plug will recognize the animal depicted in this chapter, and hardly consider him exaggerated – but the uninitiated will feel justified in regarding his portrait as a fancy sketch, perhaps.

9 HOW HEMHOTCH SCOOPED THE POOL AT AUTEUIL

A. E. Hotchner

After Aaron Hotchner, a magazine editor, met Ernest Hemingway in Havana in 1948, the pair became close friends. Hotchner accompanied the Hemingway équipe on several visits to Europe: browsing through the 'moveable feast' that was Hemingway's Paris; playing improvised baseball in the Gritti Palace in Venice; carousing and watching corridas in Pamplona. Perhaps their happiest jaunt was a visit to Paris in the winter of 1950 when they operated their informal racing syndicate (i.e. did a lot of relaxed betting) on steeplechase races at Auteuil racecourse. Their betting put into rigorous action Hemhotch Ltd., a joke partnership that Hemingway had nonetheless formally registered in New Jersey. The company was 'dedicated to the pursuit of the steeplechase, the bulls, the wild duck and the female fandango.' Their racegoing was meant to peak when Hemingway studiously engineered an immense betting coup on a horse whom Hotchner rescued from oblivion by narrating the project in his best-selling book Papa Hemingway.

I do not expect ever to duplicate the pleasure of those Paris steeplechase days. The Degas horses and jockeys against a Renoir landscape; Ernest's silver flask, engraved 'From Mary with Love' and containing splendidly aged Calvados; the boisterous excitement of booting home a winner, the glasses zeroed on the moving point, the insistent admonitions to the jockey; the quiet intimacy of Ernest's nostalgia. 'You know, Hotch, one of the things I liked best in life was to wake early in the morning with the birds singing and the windows open and the sound of horses jumping.' We were sitting on the top steps of the grandstand, the weather damp, Ernest wrapped in his big trench coat, a knitted tan skullcap on his head, his beard close-cropped. We had eaten lunch at the course restaurant: Belon oysters, omelette with ham and fine herbs, cooked endives, Pont-l'Evêque cheese and cold Sancerre wine. We were not betting the seventh race and Ernest was leaning forward, a pair of rented binoculars swinging from his neck, watching the horses slowly serpentine on to the track from the paddock.

'When I was young here,' he said, 'I was the only outsider who was allowed into the private training grounds at Achères, outside of Maisons-Laffitte, and Chantilly. They let me clock the workouts – almost no one but owners were allowed to operate a stop-watch – and it gave me a big jump on my bets. That's how I came to know about Epinard. A trainer named J. Patrick, an expatriate American who had been a friend of mine since the time we were both kids in the Italian army, told me that Gene Leigh had a colt that might be the horse of the century. Those were Patrick's words, "the horse of the century".

'He said, "Ernie, he's the son of Badajoz-Epine Blanche, by Rockminster, and nothing like him has been seen in France since the days of Gladiateur and La Grande Ecurie. So take my advice – beg, borrow or steal all the cash you can get your hands on and get it down on this two-year-old for the first start. After that there'll never be odds again. But that first start, before they know that name, get down on him".

'It was my "complete poverty" period – I didn't even have milk money for Bumby, but I followed Patrick's advice. I hit everyone for cash. I even borrowed a thousand francs from my barber. I accosted strangers. There wasn't a sou in Paris that hadn't been nailed down that I didn't solicit; so I was really "on" Epinard when he started in the Prix Yacoulef at Deauville for his debut. His price was fifty-nine to ten. He won in a breeze, and I was able to support myself for six or eight months on the winnings.'

. . . (Ernest continued), 'The old Enghien (course) – the antique, rustic, conniving Enghien before they rebuilt the stands in *pesage* and *pelouse* and all that unfriendly concrete – that was my all-time favorite track. It had a relaxed, unbuttoned atmosphere. One of the last times I went there – I remember it was with Evan Shipman, who was a professional handicapper as well as a writer, and Harold Stearns, who was "Peter Pickum" for the Parish edition of the Chicago *Tribune* at the time – Harold and Evan were relying on form and drew a blank on the day's card. I hit six winners out of eight. Harold was rather testy about my wins and asked me for the secret of my success. "It was easy," I told him. "I went down to the paddock between races, and I smelled them." The truth is, where horses are concerned, the nose will triumph over science and reason every time.'

He took the racing form out of his pocket and studied it a moment. 'This is the true art of fiction,' he said. 'Well, we haven't done very well today. I wish I still had my nose, but I can't trust it any more. I can trace the decline of my infallible-nose period to the day John Dos Passos and I came out to this track to make our winter stake. We were both working on books and we needed enough cash to get us through the winter. I had touted Dos on to my paddock-sniffing as a sure thing and we had pooled everything we had. One of the horses in the seventh race smelled especially good to me, so we put our whole stake on him. He fell at the first jump. We didn't have a sou in our pockets and had to walk all the way back to the Left Bank from here.'

The last week of the Auteuil meet we audited the Hemhotch books and found we were running slightly ahead, but considering the time, skill, emotion and energy which had gone into our Steeplechase Devotional, 'slightly' was hardly proper compensation. Two days before the end of the meet, however, on December 21 to be exact, as it sometimes happens to horse players, our fortunes dramatically surged upwards.

It began with a phone call at six in the morning.

'This is Hemingstein the Tout. Are you awake?'

'No.'

'Then get awake. This is a big day. I have just had word from Georges that there is a good horse in today's race, the first one that Georges really believes in, and I think we better meet earlier than usual and give it our special attention.' Ernest was referring to Georges, the Ritz's *chef du bar*, who was a very cautious track scholar, so this development had to be treated seriously.

The Ritz's elevator lights up '*entendu*' when you press the button, which was also my reaction to being summoned to this urgent meeting. Ernest was in his old wool bathrobe, secured, naturally, with the GOTT MIT UNS belt, sitting at a small antique desk, already at work on some form sheets. 'When Georges called at six,' he told me, 'I'd already been up a couple of hours. I got up at first light because I was dreaming the actual stuff – it sometimes happens to me – dreaming the actual lines, so had to get up to write it down or would have dreamed it all out. Closed the bathroom door and sat on the can and wrote it down on toilet paper so as not to wake Mary.'

'You better get dressed, lamb,' Mary said.

Ernest told me that the name of the horse was Bataclan II, that the word was that he had previously performed under wraps but was now going to be given its head for the first time; the odds were twenty-seven to one. He had already gathered and studied every available piece of information about Bataclan's past performances, had checked him out favourably with his jockey-room contacts, and had come to the conclusion that we should shoot the entire contents of our treasury and whatever other capital we could raise on the nose of this jumper.

. . . My Paris sources for steeplechase fund-raising were, to say the least, limited, but by the time I checked in at the Ritz Bar at the appointed hour, I had managed to scrounge some additional capital from a former girl friend, an old Air Force buddy who now worked at the transportation desk of American Express, the play-writing (non-produced) wife of a French publisher, a young lyric soprano I knew who sang at the Opera, the proprietor of a *bistro* where I was an established eater, and the business manager of *Newsweek*, to whom I had sold my French Ford when I left Paris in 1947. I had never solicited funds before and I felt like one of those small round women who shake cans at Broadway theatre intermissions. I also felt the ghost of young John Dos Passos sitting heavily on my shoulder.

Ernest was deep in consultation with Georges when I arrived. Bloody Marys to one side, the table top was a morass of charts, forms, scribbles and whatnot. The 'thorough briefing' was one of Ernest's most salient characteristics, and it applied to everything he did. His curiosity and sense of pursuit would send him swimming through schools of minutiae which would flow into his maw and emerge crystallized on the pages of *Death in the Afternoon* or *Big Two-Hearted River* or in his flawless techniques for deep-sea fishing and big-game hunting. Now he was in pursuit of Bataclan II.

Apologetically I placed my rather meagre collection of franc notes on the table. Ernest pulled a sheet of paper out from under the others and added my amount to a list. 'We have more contributors,' he said 'than a numbers drop in the Theresa Hotel on a Saturday afternoon. Every waiter in the joint has something down, plus Georges, plus Bertin, Claude the groom, and Maurice the men's-room attendant. If Bataclan doesn't perform as expected, we better check into another hotel tonight.'

(Ernest) was interrupted, this time by the arrival of a short plump man in clerical robes who called out, 'Don Ernesto!'

'Black Priest!' Ernest exclaimed, and he arose and embraced him Spanish-fashion. Black Priest, on a month's sabbatical, had arrived in Paris on his way to a little town in the north of France where he was about to invest his modest life's savings in a new ceramic factory that was being started by a Frenchman he had met in Cuba. He had some reservations about the trustworthiness of his new partner, as did Ernest, but Black Priest felt it was worth the risk since it was his only chance of emancipation. He sat at the table and drank a Bloody Mary and watched in wonderment as Ernest wound up our pre-track conference with a final audit of the funds to be bet. 'I'm sorry to have to run off, Black Priest,' Ernest said, 'but we have this titanic track venture under way. Please have dinner with us tonight at eight o'clock.'

'Don Ernesto,' Black Priest said solemnly in Spanish, 'I have been listening to the nature of your operation, and I would like to come to the track with you and invest my ceramic money in your race horse instead.'

'I'm sorry,' Ernest answered in Spanish, 'but I could not accept the responsibility for such a risk.'

A rather heated discussion followed, Black Priest insisting, Ernest refusing, until a compromise was reached that Black Priest was to bet only half his ceramic money on Bataclan II.

As we moved towards the door, Ernest said to me, 'I better take my lucky piece now.' We always took each other's responsibleness for granted. 'It fell on my head,' I said, 'where the Champs Elysées comes into the Concorde. It has a nice clear eye, don't you think?'

Ernest took the chestnut, examined it, rubbed some oil on it from the side of his nose, nodded, and put it in his pants pocket. 'Never lose your faith in mysticism, boy,' he said, and he pushed on through the revolving door.

Ernest went down to the paddock and studied our horse and the other horses as they paraded by; later, when we were in the grandstand and Bataclan came on to the track, he said, 'The ones we have to worry about are Klipper and Killibi. That Killibi has a good smell. But, as you know, the thing that really spooks me is that goddam last jump.'

The cockney-speaking tout and his pal, whom we had previously encountered, now approached Ernest and offered him a guaranteed, certified mount, but he demurred. I waited until the last moment to get our bets down; we were betting so heavy I didn't want the tote board to show it before closing. The final odds were nineteen to one. I got back to the stands just as the horses broke away. Bataclan ran first, then faded to second on the upgraded backstretch; he lost more ground on the water jump, and on the turn it was Killibi, Klipper and Bataclan in that order. As they came towards us going into the last jump, Bataclan was a hopeless twenty lengths off the pace. I moaned. 'Keep your glasses on them,' Ernest commanded.

As Killibi took the low hedge, pressed by Klipper, his jockey reached for the bat and in so doing loosened his grip, Killibi's front legs dropped slightly and scraped the hedge, breaking his stride, and he hit the turf hard and stumbled and pitched forwards with his boy jumping clear. Klipper was already through the jump at the fall; his jockey tried to clear the fallen Killibi but he couldn't make it and Klipper went right down on top of Killibi, the jock hitting the turf hard and not moving.

Bataclan's jockey had plenty of time to see what had happened and he took Bataclan to the opposite side of the hedge for his jump and came in five lengths to the good.

Nobody in our party made any effort to subdue his feelings. We started a jubilant exodus to the bar, but along the way Black Priest suddenly stopped and refused to budge. He just stood there, looking determined. 'Not yet,' he kept saying. 'Not yet.' When the stands around us had emptied, he gave a quick look around and then moved his foot off a Bataclan win ticket it had been covering. 'No doubt about it,' Ernest said, 'God is everywhere.'

I took all tickets to the cashier while the others went off to the bar for champagne, and what I returned with was a Matterhorn of ten-thousand-franc notes. Ernest peeled off Black Priest's winnings and gave it to him. 'Black Priest needs bird in hand,' he said. 'He's been in the bush too long.'

As always Ernest was wearing his special race-track jacket, a heavy tweed coat that had been made for him when he was in Hong Kong, and which contained a very deep inside pocket that had an elaborate series of buttons which reputedly made it pickpocket proof, even by Hong Kong standards. Into it he stuffed all our loot and it made him look like a side-pregnant bear. As Ernest was stacking the money, the two touts who had approached us earlier went by. 'Ah,' one of them said to Ernest, tipping his hat, 'one can see that Monsieur is of the *métier*.'

Black Priest stood at one end of the bar, his eyes aglow, his winning wad grasped in his left hand, while his right forefinger lovingly counted the money. At this moment a man, in passing, raised his hat and said 'Good evening, Father,' and Black Priest, not taking his eyes off the money, made a quick sign of the cross with his money-counting forefinger and then immediately put it back to work.

10 EVENTING
The toughest test of horse and rider

Richard Meade

Courage, dedication, enterprise, sacrifice, timely luck – these are among the main qualities needed for success in three-day eventing. Olympic gold medallist Richard Meade, who wrote the following article, has them all. Plus another vital factor. In choosing eventing, which he describes as the most demanding of all horse sports, Mr Meade was lucky that he was born an Englishman. For practical reasons (climate, fox-hunting traditions, its enormous population of active horse riders), England is the finest country of all for potential eventing champions. Results in international competitions keep on proving this.

England holds another and unique asset; the truly phenomenal public awareness of eventing and another once-arcane sport, show jumping. People who don't live there could never comprehend the popularity of these sports. On television, show jumping programmes can attract viewing audiences of ten million and beyond (second only to association football); the sport's biggest events command large chunks of newspaper space; more than 120,000 spectators will turn up to see an eventing programme. In a competition based on famous couples (Laurel & Hardy, Morecambe & Wise, etc.), a washing-powder company included one of show jumping's most famous pairs, Anne Moore and her horse Psalm. This would be unthinkable elsewhere but was acceptable for millions of British washday toilers who had never ridden anything friskier than a merry-go-round horse.

As an eventing champion, Richard Meade is a national figure. In any other country he would still have the talent and the medals but would regrettably be much closer to the renowned anonymity of gold medallist javelin throwers and long-distance walkers. As he himself acknowledges, luck is so important.

But for a piece of luck, or coincidence, I might never have followed a career in three-day-eventing and had the opportunity of winning Olympic gold medals for my country. Just after Christmas in 1961 I went to stay with friends in the village of Celbridge in County Kildare, Ireland. Although this was to be a foxhunting trip, the holiday had more serious overtones:

I was looking for a horse to train for a place in the British team for the Tokyo Olympics, less than three years away. Unless I found a promising horse quickly, my prospects would be slender. For fifteen months I had been nurturing a strong ambition to ride for Britain, an ambition that had kindled while I watched the eventing competition as a mere spectator at the Olympic Games in Rome. Perhaps I should say re-kindled, because the resolve had first stirred in me back in 1954 when, at the age of fifteen, I had successfully ridden one of Colonel Harry Llewellyn's horses in Pony Club championships. On my return from Rome, I set about finding the right horse as quickly as my studies at Cambridge University and other commitments would allow.

In Kildare, my friends had advertised for a suitable horse before my arrival. They had received nine replies, of which none produced anything suitable. But then, from their own village appeared Barberry, a raw seven-year-old who had done just a bit of hunting and a little show jumping. At the precise moment I needed a lucky break, he came along out of the blue.

Through the kindness of Colonel V. D. S. Williams and his wife, two marvellous benefactors of British equestrian sports, I spent the whole of the summer vacation of 1962 having lessons at their home near Slough, close to London. Then things began to click into place and two years later, after the inevitable setbacks which at some stage beset anyone aiming for an Olympic team, I joined the squad for Tokyo. In those Games I came eighth in the individual event after being in the lead at the end of the cross-country. Alas, we came to pieces in the show jumping, floundering in very wet conditions that Barberry was not experienced enough to handle and nor, for that matter, was I. The next year I rode him in the British team which came third in the 1965 European Championships in Moscow. The following one we were second in the individual title at the World Championships at Burghley. Quick-witted and immensely brave, he had been the perfect horse for the young and inexperienced rider I was when he came unexpectedly and, as it turned out, so fortunately into my life. I feel that if Barberry had not appeared when he did in 1962 I would not be riding competitively now.

During the mid-sixties, Barberry was generally regarded as the best three-day-event horse in the world but a back injury at the final trial before the Mexico Olympics in the autumn of 1968 ended his competitive life. The most thrilling moment of my career came at these Games when Britain, after several years in the doldrums, won the team gold medal and Major Derek Allhusen the individual silver. Four years later I was the only survivor of that winning team when Britain defended the title at Munich. The pressure was really on, the opposition stronger than ever and, in the end the team gold was ours and I was fortunate enough to win the individual title as well on Derek Allhusen's Laurieston.

The following year I set about finding a horse for the 1976 Olympics in Montreal. This proved a much harder task than it had been eleven years earlier. I combed England and Ireland for a whole year before I settled for Jacob Jones. Then another eleven months of diligent searching went by until a second horse appeared on the scene, Tommy Buck. For almost four months before finding Tommy Buck I had been looking at two or three horses every weekend. Both horses were to be eight years old in 1976, a little too young perhaps for the greatest honours – but then Laurieston was eight in Munich. Ideally an eventing horse is at his best from nine to twelve years of age. But, as long as things don't go really wrong, I believed both Jacob Jones and Tommy Buck could really have a great future.

My own future I would consider when I thought it opportune to do so. I have always regarded each Olympic Games as an end in itself. After each one I have thought carefully about the future. If you get to the top it is much better to retire while you are still there. Apart from anything else, with horses the top is a precarious place. You can have the best horse in the world, have your training programme progressing perfectly, then walk into his stable one morning to find him on three legs. Months, or years, of training can have hobbled away overnight.

After thirteen years of international competition, I feel I am still learning constantly: I have never felt at any stage of any competition that I am over the top. Assuming I have the time and the horses are there, I see no reason why I should not try for the 1980 Olympics in Moscow. What would make me stop are my business commitments as a financial planning consultant. If I couldn't devote enough time to keep on top of the sport, I would have to give up. It is no good stepping aside for a year or two, then attempting to come back. Competition is far too tough for that.

A sport is healthy when it keeps progressing. In the Britain of the mid-1970s, eventing is very healthy indeed, and its popularity is growing faster than ever in the United States; their world championship win in 1974 has seen to that, and it is flourishing also in Canada, Australia, South Africa and in Europe.

A healthy sport must also have a broad base, with a great many people interested in it at its grass-roots. In Britain there are more than two million riders, many of them belonging to pony and riding clubs. There is an abundance of one-day events which have the ingredients of dressage, show jumping and cross country, all in that one day. This is a splendid state of affairs. In addition to the broad base there must also be some stars who will inspire youngsters to take up the sport and then give them a goal to aim for; Britain has benefited from her regular successes in international competitions. Then the media must bring the sport to the public, and here Britain scores once again. Three-day-eventing was little-known until Badminton was first televised around the mid-1960s, thereby giving millions of viewers their first glimpse and taste for it. To everyone's benefit, television presentation has improved considerably since those early days.

There is no doubt that our gold medal win at Mexico in 1968 in the most appalling climatic conditions made a tremendous impression. Four and a half inches of rain fell in seventy-five minutes during the cross country phase. People who had watched highlights on television were talking about it when I returned home. Some people from Monmouthshire, my home county, who had never been over the next hill, were enthusing about eventing in Mexico as if it had taken place in a neighbouring village. The public imagination had been fired and, what is more, people were beginning to realise that eventing is a different sport from show jumping.

The structure of the sport is sound, and, inside it, techniques keep improving. The standard of riding, and therefore competition, is higher than it has ever been. Youngsters coming into the sport receive far better and more expert help than was available when I started.

It is almost impossible nowadays for any competitor to reach for, and stay at, the pinnacle of a sport if pinned down by a full-time, nine-to-five job during the week. You can, however, climb to the top while working, or averaging, eight hours work a day. The crucial factor is being able to arrange those hours so that you can train at the best time of day. Luckily, I have been able to gear my work to allow me the fullest and best training periods. Without such flexibility, I could not hope to continue riding at international level. I must admit that at times I have sacrificed a degree of attainment in business to continue my riding career.

All this effort makes for a very full, taxing but exciting life. To sustain the required effort of pursuing two careers simultaneously, a person must have a great deal of inner drive. I believe I have strong competitive instincts: if I am going to indulge in any activity I want to do it well. And I am competitive in riding above anything else. My ambitions are clearcut: I ride to compete and when I am schooling, I am preparing a horse, or horses, for the next competition, be it a small one up the road, Badminton, Burghley or the Olympic Games.

I must have a goal, and that next competition provides it. Living in Kensington, in central London, I have no facilities near at hand. I base my horses at one of three places within an hour's drive of the capital. I readily undertake that journey to prepare the horses for the next competition and to receive technical help from friends in dressage and jumping. It would be pointless to spend so much time travelling for recreational riding alone. The competitive urge is there and it has not changed much since those early days of riding in pony club gymkhana events. I was blowed then if I was going to be the one without a pole to hang his hat on!

I delight in taking on the dual challenge that three-day-eventing holds for me: the course itself and the opposing riders. The order is significant: it is not so much beating the opposition that matters as dealing with the course, jumping it clear and fast. When I am competing, the opposition seldom enters my mind. Plenty of mistakes will be made during any competition; if you can avoid making any, which means focussing entirely on the course, you are in with a chance.

When I was a youngster it was the challenge, and exhilaration, of riding at a fence at the gallop; of racing across great open spaces; of having to use initiative on the cross country, that attracted me to eventing above show jumping. While being most enjoyable, show jumping is more controlled and precise; it does not have as wide a range of pleasures, or tests, for the horseman. Besides, as a specialist sport, show jumping was virtually a full-time job, even in the more leisurely days when I began riding. The season now lasts nearly the whole year round and I could never have devoted all the time it needs to reach the top.

The advantage of eventing is that it is a non-specialist branch of equestrian sports; it is for all-rounders. The French call it *Le Concours Complet* and the Italians *Il Concorso Completo*. These titles come closest to describing what the sport is about: it is indeed the complete test of horse and rider. The British title of three-day event is not very satisfactory. It is not descriptive, gives no clue that the sport involves horses at all and, more often than not, the event lasts four days, not three!

The uninitiated find it hard to understand what is involved in a competition spread over several days and a large area of land. Many people who have watched the speed and endurance phase know it merely as the cross-country day; they see the horse and rider only on the last section of the course. They don't realise the competitors have already done three phases totalling up to twenty-four kilometres. Phases A and C are roads and tracks covered at a speed of 240 metres a minute, or 14.4 kilometres an hour. Phase B is the steeplechase course of up to four kilometres (2.5 miles), to be ridden at the near-racing speed of 600 metres a minute (36 k.p.h.). Then, after only a ten-minute break, horse and rider start on the last part, Phase D. This can be up to 8 kilometres long with thirty to thirty-five fences. They are solid and built to use the terrain and natural features, such as hills, banks, ditches, water and quarries. By the end of that day, horse and rider have completed about 32 kilometres.

On the final day, the horse must show he can still perform; that he is not too exhausted from the rigours of the previous day. He has to negotiate a fairly simple course of show jumps. So during three to four days the same horse has been asked to do a dressage test, tackle every conceivable type of obstacle across country and still jump cleanly and accurately on the last day. For me the sport has five distinctive phases: dressage, roads and tracks, steeplechasing, cross country and show jumping. Each phase involves a different balance of horse and rider, different paces and different priorities.

You must train for each phase, and the horse must be equally at home in all. In training, judgment is crucial: every horse and trainer has to aim at achieving the right balance in preparing for each phase. So it is easy to see why this is truly the pentathlon of equestrian sports.

It is the toughest sport man has ever devised for the horse; any weakness is likely to be found out. The three-day horse must have many qualities: good confirmation of limbs; a long, flowing stride; a gallop to propel him over rough and awkward ground with minimal effort; a good jump and courage. A young horse with good spirit and temperament, and a natural talent over small fences can be trained up to tackling championship fences if he has the right athletic ability, and enough trust in his rider.

Some twenty years ago, opinion held sway in Britain that a courageous rider on a good English Thoroughbred could win any three-day event on a second day's performance alone. Dressage was thought to be a necessary evil that only foreigners bothered about. A number of dressage-oriented trainers at that time held the counter view: jumping was merely an elongation of a horse's canter stride; therefore a horse drilled and obedient, with a high degree of dressage training should have no worries with the other phases. To these people, only dressage mattered.

Perhaps in those days the British were better mounted than most other Europeans. But times have changed. Nowadays, even the average horse at any C.C.I. (*Concours Complet International*) is a fine stamp, and each year his quality improves. Competition is now such that the rider must prepare himself and his horse to the highest possible standard in every phase of the competition.

From the moment an experienced horse comes in from a rest at grass, I try to allow three-and-a-half months in which to prepare him for a three-day event. During the first month, he will do long, slow work, walking and trotting up to two hours a day on roads to harden off his legs. In the second month I cut down road work and gradually build up dressage to a maximum of forty-five minutes on any one day. After two weeks of dressage, I will start gymnastic training over cavaletti and grids. At this stage, out hacking I try to make the most of any available hills to make him 'blow' a bit. This develops his breathing, clears his wind and increases his pulse rate to ensure a gradual inprovement in his fitness.

By the third month he is ready to start fast work. I will work him on gallops at least once a week, sometimes twice. By this time, I have reduced the slow hacking to between fifteen and thirty minutes a day. However, the overall work pattern must be geared to each individual horse. It also depends on the facilities available, the state of the ground, the hills and the climate. And, for an amateur, the most difficult factor of all: time. As a general rule, two hours a day is more than enough; often an hour and a half will do. Jumping on unlevel or hilly ground puts more strain on the horse's limbs

Facing:
In and out of the water: nerve, stamina, and cool judgement are all ingredients of Richard Meade's supreme horsemanship.

Over page:
Lieutenant General Sir Harry Chauvel G.O.C. Desert Mounted Corps leading his troops into Damascus after they had captured it for the allies.

A master of dressage, Richard Meade relishing the magnificent discipline of a Lippizaner at the Spanish Riding School in Vienna.

Facing:
Lord Patrick Beresford (*right*) has gained the edge on rivals, Prince Charles (*second from left*) and Mark Vestey (*centre*) in the 1974 Horse & Hound Cup.

than jumping on the flat. So I usually confine cross-country schooling to the third month, when the horse is fairly fit. After three months he will be, I hope, in almost peak condition. The remaining fortnight I have budgeted as injury time.

It is important to be flexible in our approach to training horses. We must never forget that, just as we are individuals, so are they. This applies especially to feeding. One year, in preparing two horses for Badminton, I was feeding one with eighteen pounds of oats and, in addition, some high-protein horse cubes; the other was having eight pounds of oats and low-protein cubes. Feeding must always be geared to the horse's mental and physical state and the work he is doing.

Before World War II, most cavalry schools throughout Europe concentraten on classical dressage and show jumping, while the British chased foxes, raced and played polo. British horsemen were practical but their standards were far below those on the continent in theory, style and the finer points of riding. After the war cavalry regiments were dissolved. Many instructors from mainland Europe emigrated to build careers in the 'unenlightened' countries of Britain, Canada, the United States, Australia and South Africa. The dressage and show jumping oriented countries soon realised that they had to train something better than the halfbred or the troop horse to compete with near-thoroughbreds.

The best amateur sportsmen end up with no vacant shelf-space. An immaculate Richard Meade has won the 1970 Horseman of the Year Award and a lively chat with the Queen Mother.

Technical knowledge percolated among countries; standards of eventing horses improved and levelled out. Course building became more scientific, especially in the 1960s and 1970s, with more fences introduced to test the rider's as well as the horse's ability. Television helped to promote a keenness so strong (in Britain at least) that riders sacrificed other pleasures to cope with cruelly increased costs that nearly doubled between 1974 and 1976.

The brilliant heritage of foxhunting has been one of the strengths in producing eventing riders in Britain. It builds initiative in both horse and rider; gives them a sixth sense about going across country. Horses, being gregarious animals, adore it. In practical terms, hunting helps a horse to develop a 'fifth leg', that ability to adjust and stay on his feet after a bad mistake. He learns to tackle anything, to look after himself when tired, and to build the stamina he will need at the end of a long and gruelling cross country course. The horse has a strong sense of self preservation and I believe the rider must develop the same. He must be able to anticipate problems before they occur and react in order to prevent their happening. Hunting helps to develop this.

Some people are terrified of the dangers they perceive in eventing. I think you have to be fatalistic if you ride. Life itself is dangerous and we all have to cross a road some time or another. You can't allow the spectre of danger to intrude on your thoughts.

It seems to me that people don't take up three-day eventing for logical reasons. It can be expensive, savagely demanding and bring little or no financial return. It is a crazy, but exhilarating, sport full of challenges, opportunities, frustrations and disappointments. Furthermore, it occupies a lot of time; it has occupied a lot of my time. But I don't regret a second of it. The horse world has long been a part of my life . . . and I will always be involved in it somehow.

11 POLO
The fastest game in the world

Lord Patrick Beresford

For those who rejoice in a ball struck cleanly, and in the courage of a horse in combat, there is no parallel to polo. It is the fastest game in the world and naturally possesses that small but alluring element of danger without which no pastime is wholly satisfying. It is truly international, and is practised today in at least sixty countries around the globe, from the Caucasus to the Caribbean, from Arab Emirates to South Pacific islands, and from Hong Kong to newly-independent African nations. Four centuries ago Akbar the Great described it as 'the game to test a man and to strengthen the ties of friendship,' and despite many far from friendly exchanges between irate polo players since then, the wisdom of his comment is now more than ever apparent. The constant wanderlust of players has formed a world-wide brotherhood, whose stars, and the countries from which they come, are the subject of this article.

Originally created in Persia as long ago as 600 B.C., polo was brought to the Western world in 1869 by British cavalry officers returning from India's North-West frontier. They introduced certain refinements, such as rules: one was to substitute a circular willow-root ball for the human skull or whatever else had previously been used; another was to reduce the number of players on each side from the entire male population of a village to a mere six and, later, to only four.

The precepts established then have remained virtually unchanged ever since, except for the cancellation of a 58-inch height limit on ponies and an off-side clause, both of which had tended to slow down and bunch up the play.

From England the game spread quickly to the Continent, to the United States, and to South America, and in the land of the gaucho it found a natural habitat. But, apart from Argentina, where the sport has reached a zenith and crowds of thirty to forty thousand pack Buenos Aires's giant

Seymour Hill, the brilliant Australian, showing why he is considered to have the widest repertoire of strokes among modern polo players.

Palermo stadium, the polo community in most countries is quite small. In England – still probably the world's third-strongest polo power – there are less than twenty clubs containing only about 500 playing members altogether. For this reason the arrival of a visitor or more especially of a visiting team is a welcome stimulus to local players and spectators alike. To those who play, and who wish to follow the sun an opportunity is thus afforded of world-wide travel and a key to many doors which would otherwise remain closed.

Polo has another special charm. Because teams are generally matched according to the aggregate handicap of individuals (varying from a beginner's minus 2 to an optimum of 10), players of modest ability often find themselves competing with seasoned international performers. In tennis, for example, no novice expects to partner Arthur Ashe against the service of Rod Laver, yet in polo the equivalent is almost commonplace.

Against every probability the game was successfully revived in England after World War II by determined men. Foremost among them was the gallant Lord Cowdray, a pre-war player of considerable promise who had tragically lost an arm at Dunkirk, and the energetic Prince Philip, whose enthusiasm did much not only to popularise the sport but also to influence it in a profoundly beneficial and progressive way. Though his participation was a form of mental relaxation from more important matters, Prince Philip rode as hard and as fearlessly as the best, yet carried from the field none of the rancour which sometimes disfigures the game. For him the whistle that ended a match also extinguished any discord or disagreement that the heat of the moment had ignited. Refreshingly, therefore, he rose above the feuds and vendettas which personal ambition and financial involvement all too often create. Furthermore, his original and realistic thinking inspired many innovations unconsidered by those so deeply involved that they had lost the perspective of an independent and common-sense approach. Throughout the 1960s Prince Philip was, at a five-goal handicap, one of the top four English players, and his retirement in 1971 because of an arthritic wrist left a gap in the ranks which can only be filled by the highly-talented Prince Charles, if and when polo can be slotted regularly into his heavy schedule of public duties.

From 1968 onwards, the strong man of Prince Philip's Windsor Park team was Paul Withers, long, lanky, hard-hitting, hard-riding and undoubtedly the most colourful figure among present-day English players. His recklessness, his frequent and spectacular falls, his injured innocence when the whistle blows against him, his imprecations in Spanish and Swahili, his sagging lip and thrusting jaw, these are characteristics which the crowd can neither condone nor totally condemn, yet invariably find compulsive to watch. For several seasons he carried the highest rating of any European, before being joined on seven goals by the Hopwood brothers from Cirences-

Prince Charles has inherited some of his father's enthusiasm for polo. Here he is in action at Smith's Lawn, Windsor Great Park 1976.

84

ter. Julian (since raised to handicap 8) and Howard are both blessed with the natural eye and ability that would have doubtless taken them equally far whatever ballgame they had chosen.

The only continental player of similar calibre in recent years has been the saturnine Spaniard, Perrico Domecq, from the renowned firm of sherry producers. His family have long been a formidable force in their country's major tournaments. The most important of these is the King's Cup, held during June in Madrid, which, at a ceiling of 25 goals, is the best polo available in Europe and which attracts many high-handicap Latin Americans, especially the Mexicans.

For more than thirty years polo in Mexico was synonymous with the name of Gracida, the family from which came the four brothers, Chino, Cano, Memo and Pato, who, in the manner of 17th-century buccaneers, plundered silver from both sides of the Atlantic. As boys their equitational prowess caught the eye of the polo-crazy President Avilla Commacho, by whom they were swiftly commissioned into the army. Thereafter they soon formed a national team capable of competing in the late 1940s on almost level terms with the United States. Indeed, in one tournament, they might even have extended Argentina had not one brother been obliged to flee Buenos Aires to avoid becoming the victim of a 'crime passionel'. Time has inevitably dimmed the light that once burned so brightly for the Gracidas, and their place has been taken by the professionals Antonio Herrera and Javier Rodriguez, and by Pablo Rincon Gallardo, whose father Jaime breeds the finest polo ponies in Central America.

These superb animals are raised on the mountainous pastures of his *estancia* four hundred miles north of Mexico City. Both their sires and dams have generally played polo and are of thoroughbred or almost thoroughbred stock. They are introduced to the game with unhurried patience and understanding and are in constant demand on both sides of the border.

Another country fortunate enough to have no need to import ponies is South Africa, where racehorses which have proved too small for the track are brilliantly retrained for polo. Most of the local players are strong silent farmers of both Afrikaan and British stock. As one battered visitor remarked, 'they are quarried not born' and their handshakes are indeed akin to the embrace of a mobile stone-crusher. In complete contrast are the flamboyant Goodman twins from Johannesburg, identical in every respect from the tips of their meticulously-waxed moustaches to the toes of their gleaming boots. It is impossible to imagine anyone extracting more zest from life, and especially from polo, than these two charming extroverts, aptly described as 'magnificent peacocks' in the autobiography of Zsa Zsa Gabor, whose experienced eye had lit on one of them at a tournament in Deauville.

The quality of exuberance is sadly diminished in India, formerly the cradle of the game but now, through the disbandment of the Maharajas and the redistribution of their lands, more like its graveyard. Gone are many of the lightning-fast polo fields, once the scene of the most artistic and inspiring games the world has known, when private strings numbered up to sixty strong, each pony magnificently prepared by its own individual groom. By the mid-1970s there were very few players other than the officers of the only surviving mounted regiment, the 61st Cavalry stationed in Delhi.

The most talented of their number is Major V. P. Singh, whose effortless style and graceful horsemanship bring a surface reflection of a former Colonel-in-Chief, the late and legendary Maharaja of Jaipur. 'Jai', as he was popularly nick-named, and the equally unforgettable Rao Rajah Hanut Singh used to add an annual glint of oriental splendour to the English season; their invincible team of the 1930s has, for a generation, warmed and stirred the memories of aficionados lucky enough to have seen them. The team delighted spectators with the perfection of their stick-work, the delicate accuracy of their passing, and their silken fluency built on speed and finesse rather than physical strength and power.

Many of the ponies playing in India between the wars were 'Walers' imported from New South Wales. This eastern Australian state was the home of the Ashton brothers, a quartet whose intuitive understanding of each other guided their Goulburn team to frequent triumphs over sides of far greater handicap, as in the English Championship Cup of 1937. They also helped coax to greatness the then youthful Bob Skene, later to become one of the finest players in the history of polo. Born in Assam of Scottish parents, he was brought up in Tasmania and first represented England in the Westchester Cup of 1939. Having overcome the debilitation of four years in a Japanese prisoner-of-war camp, he returned to international polo in 1949 with the English team in Argentina, then going back there in 1954 and 1956 to win the Open on both occasions – the only non-Argentinian ever to do so. Now resident in Santa Barbara (California), and retired from active competition, Bob Skene devotes his life to coaching young players throughout the world.

The only contemporary non-Argentinian ten-goaler also comes from New South Wales. His name is Sinclair Hill. In 1963 he captained a young British team that crossed the Atlantic to contest the United States National 25 goal Handicap. Because Hill's Australian rating (then 8) was almost double that of his nearest rival at home (then 5), many sceptics doubted whether he could deal with American opponents who were, on paper, of equal or superior calibre. He proved them utterly wrong. By sheer application and study he had introduced to his armoury as powerful and as complete a range of strokes as had ever been seen. Moreover no captain could have better exemplified his own theories by his personal performance on the field, nor better leavened the acid of criticism with the honey of praise. He played with but one object in mind: his team must win. And win they did, returning

It seems that Eduardo Moore, of Cowdray Park, will have to square cut at the ball to make contact. Teammate H. Barrantes (*left*) and Billy Linfoot are wisely giving him room for a full, free swing.

to England having taken the 25 goal Handicap, the Spectator and North American Cups, and the Robert Uihlein International Trophy.

Long before Hill, and before the sinuous Indians of the 1930s, the United States had enjoyed almost twenty years of supremacy. Hard in the wake of World War I, they wrested the mantle from England and proved unbeatable until touched off by Argentina in 1936. Befitting a nation surging towards industrial might, the Americans injected pure power into the game – power in striking, power in aggression, even (though not surprisingly) power in spending that bought them the best in horseflesh and converted the talented cowboy into a professional player. By the 1960s polo in America had consolidated its national centres at Santa Barbara (California); Oakbrook (Illinois); and Boca Raton (Florida), with popular subsidiaries in many other states, including Oklahoma, Texas, Wisconsin and far-off Hawaii. Most of the top players were professionals, of whom the best were Harold (Chico) Barry, his nephew Roy and the dynamic Dr Billy Linfoot, all rated at nine goals.

In 1966 this trio was selected with Northrup Knox (8) to challenge Argentina for the Cup of the Americas in Buenos Aires. As soon as he stepped from the aircraft Harold Barry was dubbed with the somewhat derisive nickname of 'El Gordo' – the Fat One. Sure enough, there can never have been a polo player comparable in shape to this huge Texan, who weighed in around 300 pounds. In a U.S. Polo Association blazer that scarcely reached his quarters, he looked for all the world like a well-matured Billy Bunter. Barry contended his weight and age were a 'military secret'. The smiles of Argentinian supporters widened at the thought of what their famously-fast forwards would do to him, particularly after the preliminary games, in which he had appeared almost pitifully slow. But when the chips were finally on the table, those smiles quickly vanished.

This American team was certainly an odd one. Barry's nephew Roy, another big cowboy, stood six foot six inches in his socks, with the lazy drawl of a man from whom the sun had seemingly baked all energy. He was so unruffled that both times the American party were leaving their quarters at the Hurlingham Club to represent their country in the face of some 40,000 vociferous partisans, he was found in bed – fast asleep. Billy Linfoot was an utter contrast to the Barrys: short, bustling, bow-legged, and notably brisk in speech and movement. Against Argentina he had the toughest task: to contain and nullify the country's peerless idol, Juan Carlos Harriott, then and to this day 'El Mejor del Mundo' – the world's greatest player.

Inside the framework of team polo are four separate fascinating contests, wherein each player endeavours to eliminate his opposite number. The conventional method of marking a superior opponent is to chase him around the ground, disrupting his play by blocking, hooking, barging and other tactics designed to slow him down. Linfoot's plan for Harriott was infinitely

more subtle: instead of rough-house, he would offer remorseless speed in thought and action.

Since both were superbly mounted, their duel became a breath-taking battle of wits, skill and anticipation at a pace that brought the whole crowd to its feet time and again. While Linfoot was fractionally the loser, he managed to absorb much of the pressure which otherwise the two Barrys would have had to bear. They faced a twin-pronged attack: Horacio Heguy, a hawk-eyed speed merchant no bigger than an ill-fed jockey, and Gaston Dorignac, tough, tireless and a real bulldog. While Argentina won both games by four-goal margins, the sight of 'El Gordo' repeatedly overtaking the fleeting Heguy stupefied players and spectators alike. How Barry performed this miracle while conceding at least 120 pounds in weight was another of his 'military secrets', but was presumably due to a superlative combination of horsemanship and polo sense, whereby his ponies were balanced and saved for just one or two seconds of essential speed. The crowd adored him. When he remounted after a crashing fall in the first game, cheers soared from every corner of the stadium, and soon, in his shirt of turquoise hue, he became that 'last blue mountain' beyond which the Argentine forwards could seldom reach.

Yet neither the heroic deeds of the Barrys, nor of their recent successors in America, Tommy Wayman and Red Armour, can do much to make the Argentinians falter in their all-conquering stride. No other country in the world holds a supremacy in sport comparable to theirs in polo. Climate, terrain and environment are ideal. From Buenos Aires to the foothills of the Andes the land is flat and fertile. Each cattle ranch has ample room for any number of polo fields at minimal cost. The weather allows chukkas to be as regular as mealtimes; players are out in all four seasons of the year.

And most important, the vital raw material – the polo pony itself – still abounds. Mechanisation has plucked the American cowboy from his horse but the gaucho, like the pampa, goes on and on. As a result more than 1,000 ponies are exported annually from Argentina at prices up to $10,000 each; about half of them are shipped elsewhere in Latin America and to the United States, and the other half to Europe. Meanwhile the Argentinians have justly accredited no less than eight players with the maximum ten-goal rating, namely the brothers Harriott, the brothers Dorignac, the brothers Heguy, the tactically infallible Daniel Gonzales and the acrobatic Gonzalo Tanoira. Of these it is Tanoira who is considered most likely to topple the crown which Juan Carlos Harriott has worn since 1962.

National supremacy on this scale might be expected to deter other countries, whose summit of achievement, as things stand, cannot be higher than second place. In polo this has not happened, for the real heroes are not the players but the ponies. It is they who bless the sport with its compulsive attraction. Each man who has wielded a polo-stick remembers with pride and affection those that served him best. Will H. Ogilvie spoke a simple truth when he wrote on their behalf:

'Yet bridled, girthed and martingaled, and booted to the knee,
No keener are our masters for the winning goal than we.'

12 I HAVE CALLED THEE HORSE, I HAVE CREATED THEE ARAB

Stella A. Walker

In the years following the Second World War one of the more remarkable trends in the horse world has been the steady increase in popularity of the Pure-bred Arabian. This has not only occurred in the United Kingdom but in many countries all over the world and culminated in 1970 with the formation of the World Arabian Horse Organisation which now possesses twenty-six nation members.

Pure-bred studs in the British Isles rose from 234 in 1966 to over 600 by 1975. The growth in the number of Pure-bred Arabians in the United States has also been phenomenal, reaching, in 1975, a total of over 100,000. In fact over 12,000 Pure-bred foals are now registered there annually. The British Isles, with nearly 700 registered in 1975, takes second place, followed closely by Canada and Australia.

There has also, in recent years, been a considerable increase in international sales of Pure-bred Arabians. In 1954 Miss P. M. Lindsay, a Council Member of the Arab Horse Society (U.K.) and a well-known breeder, was instrumental in the arrival in England of many imported Polish bred Arabians (many had come from successful performance on the racecourse), which supplied valuable new blood lines. More recently, at the end of the 1960s, horses of fine quality from the studs now run by the Egyptian Agricultural Organisation (E.A.O.) have been exported to many parts of the world, including the United Kingdom, to the ancient stud at Marbach in Germany and in greater numbers to the United States, where the Egyptian strains have made considerable impact. In the same way the Polish Purebreds have also gone far afield and Arabian horses bred in Spain have been imported into England and Holland; but still the famous Crabbet blood lines perpetuated in England attract breeders from every continent. Perhaps this growing activity can be explained by the idea that a world rocked by wars and social unrest seeks an antidote in perfecting an animal of outstanding beauty. The Arabian seems uniquely fitted for this rôle with its striking presence allied to extreme elegance.

The essential characteristics of the breed have always been the dished profile of the small, wedge-shaped head with the wide forehead (the *jibbah*) and tapering muzzle, the eyes large and brilliant and placed low. The ears are small, set wide apart and strongly pricked, the neck elegantly arched. The withers are well marked, topping a short back and a level croup; the chest and ribs are wide and deep with the loins short and strong. Most noticeable is the tail, of luxuriant growth, set level with the back and held arrestingly high the instant the horse is in action. It is an unexplained fact that the Arabian generally possesses twenty-three vertebrae whereas twenty-four is the usual number for other breeds. The texture of the coat is exceptionally silky and fine, the quality of the bone is ivory hard and the hoof unusually durable. Height varies from 14 hands (142·24cms) to 15·2 hands (177·8cms). The small size of the Pure-bred Arabian obviously limits his use in some activities such as steeplechasing but it should be noted that whatever his height the Arabian is never referred to as a pony but always as a horse. Colours include chestnut, bay, brown and black and all tones of grey to white, with chestnut and grey predominating. The Arabian moves with extreme grace, trotting with a characteristic floating action. In addition, though high-spirited, he is blessed with an exceptionally kind temperament and outstanding intelligence.

It is a breed that excels in any activities demanding stamina and great endurance. In the years between 1920–22 the Arab Horse Society organized rides of 300 miles in which Pure-bred Arabian horses covered 60 miles on five consecutive days carrying, with complete equanimity, 13 stone (82·5 kilos). During the past decade the modern Quilty Cup event in Australia, open to all breeds, covers 100 miles over testing terrain. Arabians have made history by being the first home on many occasions and in fact, in 1966, of the first eight horses six were Arabian. In 1975 Noddy, a seven-eighths Arabian, won by half a minute from an Anglo-Arab mare, Ravlon Shafranna. In the similar Tevis Cup Ride in the U.S.A. in 1969 a Pure-bred Arabian covered the difficult 100 miles course in 12 hours 57 minutes saddle time to lead 144 entrants and was the third Tevis winner to be sired by the same stallion.

A 130 miles endurance race in South Africa in 1975 over three days was won by a Pure-bred mare, Elbna Nobletta. A less strenuous event, the Summer Solstice Ride over 100 miles in the New Forest in England, was won in the same year by a Pure-bred stallion, Nizzolan. These extraordinary powers of endurance and quick recuperation peculiar to the Arabian are qualities that certain breeders consider should be re-introduced into the Thoroughbred. It is an established fact that an infusion of Arabian blood into other breeds improves both stamina and quality and for these purposes it has been used over the centuries. The modern Hackney, Trakehner, Danubian, Welsh Cob, the American Standardbred, all have had, in the past, their share of Arabian blood and, of course, the Thoroughbred, a breed which has spread all over the world, owes his very existence to the prepotency of three Arabian sires.

The two derivatives of the Arabian – the Anglo-Arab and the Part-bred Arabian play a vital part in the light horse scene. The Anglo-Arab, as ruled in the British Isles, is the cross of a Thoroughbred stallion and an Arabian mare or *vice versa* – that is to say it has no strain of blood other than Thoroughbred or Arabian in its pedigree. Australia, Canada and Sweden follow this ruling but some other countries demand a certain minimum percentage of Arabian blood: in the United States not less than 25% Arabian or more than 75% Thoroughbred; in France, South Africa and the U.S.S.R. a minimum of 25% is also demanded but in Poland only $12\frac{1}{2}$%. The Anglo-Arab is a horse of great quality possessing the finest attributes of the Thoroughbred allied to the more equable temperament and intelligence of the Arabian. It performs with success as a hack, hunter, show jumper, dressage and event horse and is bred, perhaps, with greater application on the continent, especially in France, than in the United Kingdom. Such international show jumpers as P. J. D'Oriola's Olympic Gold Medal winner, Ali Baba, and Alwin Schockemöhle's Rex the Robber were both Anglo-Arabs.

Arabian blood has distinguished itself in many spheres. It flows in champion show jumper Rex the Robber, seen here at Hickstead with Alwin Schockemohle.

The Part-bred designation refers to horses other than Anglo-Arabs whose pedigrees in the British Isles contain at least 25% of Arabian blood (raised in 1974 from 12½%). Definitions again vary widely in different countries. In the United States and Canada the Part-bred is known as the Half-bred Arabian and the sire or dam must be pure Arabian, as is also required in Australia. In the British Isles it is the Part-bred which has been responsible for producing our outstanding children's ponies and it was the famous grey Arabian stallion, Naseel, bred at Hanstead, that was the sire of nine pony champions of the Dublin Spring and Summer Shows and that started a dynasty of what must be considered the world's finest show ponies. From Naseel descend such later champions as Blwch Valentino, Oakley Bubbling Spring and little Holly of Spring who swept all before him in 1975. Among those in the larger Part-bred section, horses such as Jonathan, Pasha and Shaitan have won such major Three-Day Events as Badminton and Burghley and it should not be forgotten that, though not technically a Part-bred, Miss Sheila Willcox's famous High and Mighty, twice winner at Badminton, also had an infusion of *Arabian* blood.

With some credibility the Arabian has always been considered the oldest and purest of the equine breeds and from time immemorial has been associated with romance and legend. Many of the more picturesque theories of its evolution spring from the realms of fantasy; none more graphic than its presentation as a masterpiece of divine creation as related by that philosopher and champion of Islam the Emir Abd-El-Kadir, in such versions as: 'When Allah willed to create the horse He said to the South Wind, "I will that a creature should proceed from thee – condense thyself!" – and the wind condensed itself. Then came the Angel Gabriel, who took a handful of this blessed element and presented it to Allah, who formed of it a dark bay or chestnut horse, saying, "I have called thee horse. I have created thee Arab. I have attached good fortune to the hair that falls between thine eyes. Thou shalt be the lord of all other animals. Man shall follow thee wheresoever thou goest. Good for pursuit as for flight, thou shalt fly without wings. Upon thy back shall riches repose and through thy means shall wealth come." Then he signed him with the sign of glory and of good fortune, a star in the middle of the forehead.' This story not only epitomizes the charisma that has surrounded the Arabian horse through the centuries but also serves to emphasize the fact that in more practical terms it is also a financial investment of considerable value, which is just as true today.

Various theories that have arisen about the earliest background of the breed have stemmed from deduction rather than factual scientific data. However, there is little doubt that the Arabian horse must have evolved from a single stock. Historians have long conjectured that the Arabian and also the Barb, developed gradually from the ancient Numidian horse of North-West Africa and that eventually they found a suitable environment where grasslands were interspersed with desert. But of all the hot-blooded horses of the various regions the Arabian developed into a clear-cut breed and from the earliest times it has been the Arabian which has been used to upgrade the indigenous stock of other areas, first in the countries bordering the Mediterranean, and, at a later date, further afield.

Though scientific details may be lacking clues exist in picturesque abundance borne out by early representations in rock engraving from 4,000 years ago in Syria and earlier in Spain and elsewhere. Domestication of the horse about 2500 B.C. spread from Asia Minor westwards and in Egypt, on temple bas-reliefs and on ceramic urns, the Arabian conformation makes an early appearance in the chariot teams of the Pharoahs. Legends refer to Ishmael, the horse-tamer, as the first breeder of the Arab. There is a tantalizing mention in Kings I of Solomon (who reigned in Israel from 994 to 937 B.C.) bringing horses from Egypt, which many believe was the cradle of the breed. By 300 B.C. the Arabian conformation appears on many Greek coins, which suggests that the renowned horse breeders of Thessaly also realized the value of Arabian blood.

In the Far East Chinese rulers of Chi'in and the Western Han Dynasties between 221 B.C.–A.D. 8 were receiving emissaries' accounts of horses on the western boundaries of their country in Ferghama (now Soviet Uzbestizan) which were very fast, possessed uniquely hard hooves and were considerably taller and more finely coated than their own small, coarse, surefooted ponies. The Chinese rulers sent expeditions to bring back examples of this wonder breed which were, possibly, an amalgam of Alkhal Teke, Turkoman and pure Arabian. They were designated 'celestial' and in superb Chinese pottery and bronze models of the first century B.C. they appear basically Arabian with the typical concave profile and flaunting tail.

There are many traditions relating to the Mares of the Prophet, i.e. Mahomet, (born A.D. 632), each of these narrating in different romantic form the genesis of the foundation families of the Arabian breed. Amongst those usually mentioned are Kehailan Saglawi, 'Ubayan, Hamdani, Managhi and Habdan but there are many more than these tap-roots. Dr. P. J. Gazder in his study *Arab Horse Families*, published in 1964, names nine principal strains and several minor ones.

For 2,000 years also, extravagant descriptions of the superlative attributes of the Pure-bred Arabian have varied little in content. In the first century A.D. the Arabian poet, Imra'l Qays, wrote lyrically: 'Behold then his form, stout as timber, with flanks of gazelle, legs as of ostrich, a back firm as that of a wild horse, of one standing erect on a hilltop on guard for the herd.' In 1684 John Evelyn, the diarist wrote of 'Turkish and Arabian horses' brought before Charles II in St. James's Park and indubitably pure Arabian as: 'in all regards, beautiful and proportioned to admiration; spirited, proud . . . .' In 1945 Lady Wentworth declared: 'The true Arabian has indescribable fire and pride of carriage. His movements show strength, litheness, grace and lightning quickness. His head and neck are carried high . . . his eye flashes with fire and life. His nostrils are dilated and mobile . . . he responds to every sound and dances with the joy of life.' In more mundane terms the Arab Horse Society (of the U.K.) reminds breeders in 1975: 'For centuries the Arabian horse has been renowned for presence, courage and powers of endurance, prepotency and kind temperament. These qualities still predominate today, which accounts for the ever increasing popularity of this light breed of riding horse.'

Through the centuries the cavalries of Romans, Moors and Saracens surged through Europe and Asia Minor mounted on Arab-bred horses. These became regularly established in military units in Turkey, Hungary, Spain and France. Oriental stallions were crossed with the indigenous horses of these regions from which evolved such fine breeds as the Hungarian Shagya and the Spanish Andalusian. At the end of the eighteenth century Napoleon still considered the Arabian horse 'le meilleur cheval du monde' and he seldom rode any other breed. Jaffa, Tauris and Cid are named amongst his chargers in addition to the more famous Marengo, captured at Waterloo, who finished his days at stud (not very successfully) near Newmarket.

Until the seventeenth century isolated examples of the breed had arrived in England, brought individually by the Romans, or by returning Crusaders, and had also been received as royal gifts. Later there was the highly schooled Markham Arabian, acquired by James I from the prolific equestrian writer of the age, Gervase Markham (or from one of his family) for the sum of £154, a small fortune in the currency of the day. Cromwell imported Arabians from the Middle East, his agent at Livorno also being ordered to buy horses of eastern blood from Naples and the Orient. Charles II, as recounted by John Evelyn, received three splendid stallions. That illustrious horseman, and dedicated royalist, William Cavendish, Duke of Newcastle, firmly advised that English mares should be covered by Arabian stallions as a means of producing racehorses of speed and stamina. This counsel drew strong response from the royal stud masters, wealthy sporting aristocrats and established horse breeders of Yorkshire. And from this theory evolved the wonder horse, the Thoroughbred, descended from a trio of Arabian stallions, the Byerley Turk, the Darley Arabian and the Godolphin Arabian.

Controversy has existed over the years as to the exact breeding of these three horses, as confusion arose through the custom of the times by which the port of embarkation or place of acquisition was used for the designation of Oriental horses, despite their true origins. The Byerley Turk was received as a spoil of war at Buda by Captain Robert Byerley in the campaign against the Turkish invaders and was automatically dubbed Turk though, from descriptions and illustrations, he appears to have been characteristically

The dished profile, the keen eye of the Arabian, are both splendidly shown here with Kaisoon, a grey stallion bred at El Zahraa in Egypt.

pure Arabian. Brought to England in 1689, after further military duties with his owner in Ireland at the Battle of the Boyne in the Queen Dowager's Cuirassiers, he stood in Yorkshire at Middridge and later at Goldsborough Hall and made spectacular history as a sire through the famous Herod line. The Darley Arabian of the then much-prized Managhi strain, bred in the desert of Palmyra, arrived in 1704. Imported by Mr Richard Darley, a Yorkshire country squire, he was sent by his son, Thomas, from Aleppo who wrote of the horse, 'I esteem myself happy in a colt I bought a year and a half ago . . . I believe he will not be much disliked for he is esteemed here' . . . an understatement if ever there was one of a horse that sired the Flying Childers and was the great-great-grandsire of the unbeatable Eclipse. He is particularly interesting as the Managhi line has often been denigrated by later critics. The Darley Arabian's influence on the speed and stamina of the early Thoroughbred can hardly be exaggerated. It is not only modern racing stock that traces back to this stallion but also show Hackneys, Cleveland Bays and, through Hambletonian, the Standard-breds, the famous trotting horses of America.

Prancing in the Bahrain sun, this is Kohalah Ajuz, (then 12 years old) from the stud of the Ruler H. H. Sheik Isa ben Sulman Alkhalifa.

The third progenitor of the Thoroughbred was the Godolphin Arabian brought to England in 1729 and for several years erroneously described as the Godolphin Barb from the fact that the Emperor of Morocco had presented him to the King of France. But the horse's original name was Sham (Arabic for Damascus) and in contemporary stud records he is always meticulously designated Arabian (being in fact of the Jilfan strain). He stood in the ownership of the Earl of Godolphin at Babraham near Cambridge and, through Matchem, he is the third ancestor through the male line of every living Thoroughbred.

During the eighteenth century breeders were continuing to import in increasing numbers horses from Arabia, Syria and the Lebanon. Arabian stallions certainly became a status symbol with the elite and were portrayed by all the leading animal artists of the day including John Wootton, James Seymour and the Sartorius Family; but the purpose of their owners in this country was not to further the Arabian breed as a desirable entity in itself but to use it to establish the Thoroughbred as a racehorse of outstanding capabilities. This was achieved; the Thoroughbred, quickly acquiring its own unmistakable stamp, was to make its mark all over the world, although for two or three generations, judging from contemporary portraits, the Arabian characteristics were still marked, especially the big, luminous eye and small, quality head.

To evaluate the modern Arabian it is necessary to remember that, away from the Arabian peninsula itself, the important centre of breeding for many years had been in Egypt. From the thirteenth century onwards the countries of the Lebanon, Iraq and North Africa as well as Arabia were all dominated by the Turks. Egypt was the headquarters of their provincial governments, and here and also in Tunis and Morocco local rulers first established studs for which Pure-bred Arabians were imported in some numbers from the Nejd, Iraq and Bahrein. The Sultan El Malek El Naser Mohammed Kalaon of Egypt esteemed the breed above all others and at his death in 1342 his stud numbered 3,000 horses of Arabian stock. In 1815 another important infiltration of Arabians came to Egypt when Ibrahim Pasha, nephew of Mohammed Ali, ruler of Egypt, after quelling rebellious Wahabis in the Nejd, returned with 200 of the finest Pure-breds, headed by a procession in Cairo of a dozen superlative stallions in golden trappings led by captives. In a further expedition in 1819 Ibrahim Pasha acquired for himself the entire and massive stud of the Wahabi Prince Saoud.

Thus two major studs were established in Egypt. But unfortunately at that time skilled horse-mastership played little part in Egyptian lore and with bad management and neglect the horses quickly deteriorated, were sold or given away and it was the grandson of Mohammed Ali, Abbas I, who, on becoming the first viceroy in 1832 at the age of twenty-three, re-established the Arabian in Egypt. As viceroy he was able to purchase the pick of the desert mares and stallions from the noted breeding tribes of Arabia. The prices he gave were, in the currency of the day, enormous, varying between £1,000–£7,000 for individual horses and at the end of twenty years his Abbas Pasha Sherif Stud near Cairo was outstanding and the purity of its stock beyond question. Numerous visitors reported on the beauty and quality of the horses. But in 1854 the viceroy was assassinated; his son was neither interested in nor able to finance the stud and died himself three years later. Many horses were sold, some to European countries but in addition to general maladministration the final blows were two devastating outbreaks of horse-sickness which wiped out completely several strains of the Arabian in Egypt.

At the same time, amongst the native tribes of Arabia itself, the Pure-bred native horse was deteriorating in both numbers and quality. In-breeding, over-selling of the best stock and internal Bedouin warfare were the prime factors, with the result that the continued survival of the Arabian in its own habitat became problematical. The situation was critical, for the breed had also fallen into disfavour on the continent; to fulfil increased demands mediocre half-bred stock had been misguidedly imported after the Crimean War from Syria and the Lebanon with considerable harm. A nadir had been reached.

But desperate situations find unexpected remedies. It was the attraction of the desert and its denizens for two English travellers, Wilfred Scawen Blunt, man of letters and political leader, and his wife Lady Anne, that saved the Arabian horse. Cultured and wealthy and already seasoned tourists, they journeyed in 1878 to the Near East, primarily in search of a climate suitable for Wilfred Scawen Blunt, who suffered from tuberculosis, but also to explore territory in Arabia which at that date was little known to travellers from western Europe. Fortunately this couple, with their inherent English love and understanding of horses, took a route that led them to the great horse-breeding tribes of the Nejd and the Palmyra Desert. Here they were delighted by the beauty of the few remaining horses but were appalled by their poor condition and apathy of the owners. They quickly realized the urgency of the situation if the Pure-bred Arabian was to survive. Already admirers of the breed (for a common ancestor of them both had imported Arabian stallions and mares early in the seventeenth century), on three visits to Arabia between 1878–81 they purchased several horses of the highest standard obtainable whose purity by reason of their classic conformation and their pedigrees as related by their owners, was beyond any reasonable doubt. Lady Anne Blunt, in her diaries *Bedouin Tribes of the Euphrates* and *A Pilgrimage to the Nejd*, tells how they travelled with no interpreter and often without a guide, a situation which inspired the trust of the native owners. Mutual friendship and integrity resulted in the acquisition of horses of quality. Their own Sheykh Obeyd Stud was established near Cairo, and in addition the Blunts also bought at auction in 1896 six mares and four stallions from the remnant of the celebrated stud of Viceroy Abbas I.

However, as their life was based in England there were difficulties of adequate personal supervision of the Egyptian stud and most of these horses were eventually transferred to the Blunt's home in Sussex to found the illustrious Crabbet Arabian Stud. Though other continental travellers such as Count Walsaw Rzewicki of Poland, Count S. A. Strogonoff and Prince A. G. Sherbatoff of Russia and Baron von Fechtig of Germany also journeyed east and brought back horses from the tribes of Arabia to found, or embellish, studs in their own countries, it was from the important nucleus established by the Blunts in England that the breed was to receive its most vital impetus. An all-important point recorded by Lady Anne is that the complete change of environment – of climate and feeding in particular – produced no alteration in the classic qualities of the Arabian type, but in fact their characteristics appeared even more pronounced.

On the death of the Blunts the Crabbet Stud, after a tedious lawsuit, came in 1920 into the possession of their only daughter, Lady Wentworth, and under her dynamic and perfectionist authority it became the most influential home of the Arabian horse of this century. Annual auction sales were organised by Tattersalls and attended by buyers of many nationalities. Crabbet horses were sold to numerous European countries but many also went further afield to become the foundation stock of studs in the United States of America, Australia and South Africa. Crabbet ranks as the most important source of Arabian blood in the world.

In time Lady Wentworth was in need of a suitable outcross and herself introduced an important new blood line into her stud with the Polish-bred stallion, Skowronek, imported into this country in 1913 by Mr Walter Winans, a well-known Hackney breeder, and then owned for a time by Mr H. Musgrave Clark of the renowned Courthouse Stud, before going to Crabbet. Bred by Count Potocki, Skowronek by Ibrahim, possessed a fairy-tale beauty and early in life he became nearly pure white; in addition he proved to be highly prepotent and a prolific stock getter, becoming perhaps the most important sire of this century with immense influence in the United States through his son, Raffles.

After the end of the Second World War, the death in 1956 of both Lady Wentworth and Miss Gladys Yule, owner of the Hanstead Stud (the only other dominating establishment apart from the smaller Courthouse Stud), might have heralded the decline of the Arabian breed in England. On the contrary the general disposal of top class horses was the occasion for the formation of many smaller studs and for a great upsurge of interest in the Arab.

In the following two decades the breed has reached a zenith of popularity with numbers increasing year by year. With better facilities for horse air travel, international sales are a common occurrence. Arabians from England go all over the world, but likewise stock from Poland, Egypt and the United States is in great demand. Keeping pace with this expansion, the Arab Horse Society of the U.K., formed in 1918, aims 'to preserve the pure-bred Arabian blood which already exists in the country and encourages the introduction of further specimens of the best type'. But since the mid-1960s it has also emphasized the fact that the Arabian is not only beautiful to look at and a joy to own but is also a delight to ride. It has coined the phrase: 'if you ride – ride an Arab!' The Society organizes for the breed such activities as horse and hunter trials, performance shows with show jumping, dressage, side-saddle and driving classes. A recent innovation has been a marathon race over twenty-six miles.

Some aura of romance will, perhaps, always exist about the unique attributes of the classic Arabian but basically it is a general purpose horse to be ridden and driven – a horse described by the Bedouins as 'good in all'.

13 TROUBLED TIMES
Studs in the United Kingdom

Richard Baerlein

A major problem in post-war English racing has been the drastic drop in the number of mares capable of producing horses of the highest calibre. By 1980 they could be down to less than a hundred, signalling the end of English racing as we know it.

It has been a long, long fall. First, death duties began the decline of the big owner/breeder. Then came World War II. Other fiscal measures shrivelled the ranks until the present Aga Khan remains the last of the British legendary stables – and he has virtually severed all blood stock connections with England. His grandfather, the late Aga Khan, like many other pre-war breeders, kept a colossal string of mares and horses, so many, I recall his telling me in the early 1950s, he had to win the Epsom Derby every other year to make ends meet.

Nowadays cash flow makes it impossible to retain large strings in Britain. As soon as a horse is valued at £500,000, and above, he is sold to the United States or Ireland, where facilities and circulating cash can support expensive stallions. Despite this, some owners have made gracious gestures. Paul Mellon has allowed Mill Reef to stand at the National Stud; Dr Carlo Vittadini gave similar permission for Grundy. Such concessions deserve better treatment than owners receive in Britain, where owners and breeders are bled for all manner of savage and foolish taxes. Cash flow is the eternal thorn: owners must sell horses each year at a high-enough figure to cover their outgoings or go out of business. This is an unequivocal and logical fact that dominates the thinking behind most big studs. Cliveden Stud is a good example. William Waldorf Astor (later the first Lord Astor) founded the stud in 1906. When he died in 1950, it passed to his son Bill. Warren Stud, founded in 1932, went to another son, Jakie. In 1975 Jakie Astor sold more than fifty animals at the autumn sales. Apart from two mares, this liquidated the Astor blood stock. In 1966, London property magnate Louis Freedman bought Cliveden Stud and has been trying as well as he could to restore some of its former glories.

Polygamy's 1974 win continued the stud's remarkable record in The Oaks. It was cruel luck for Freedman that Polygamy died of a twisted gut before she could produce. Mr Freedman then had to discard thoughts of selling One Over Parr (winner of the Lancashire Oaks and Cheshire Oaks), to help his cash flow. Instead he reclaimed the horse in the stud to take Polygamy's place.

After rigid culling on the lines of the old owner/breeders, Louis Freedman now has twenty-two mares permanently at Cliveden. Inevitably he must sell quality animals from time to time to keep the cash flow going until he scores with a Classic-winning colt. I believe the policy and prospects at Cliveden cannot fail to raise it back to a worldwide influence on Thoroughbred racing: Louis Freedman will continue until he runs out of money.

A swift march through Cliveden's history will show both how the English owner/breeder has declined and how money values have changed so emphatically. William Waldorf Astor was an Oxford undergraduate in 1900 when he bought the former hunter brood mare Conjure for £100, ostensibly to breed jumpers to be mated with premium stallions. By the time she became the first mare at Cliveden Stud, she had dropped seven foals, of which four were winners. Conjure died in 1921, aged twenty-six, having established one of the greatest winner-producing families in the stud book, including Oaks winners Pennycomequick and Short Story and a host of top-class colts and fillies.

Altogether Astor bought fourteen mares, which, with their progeny, achieved the stud's entire success. From 1906 until he died in 1950, Lord Astor won 550 races, earning £540,576, a figure a Dahlia or an Allez France can win these days in just four seasons' racing. Over the years, Cliveden-bred horses won the Oaks six times; the Two Thousand Guineas three times; the St Leger once and the Eclipse (then the most important race outside the Classics) four times. Astor was the most successful owner for Classics in the years 1915–40.

Jakie Astor also founded Hatley Stud at Sandy, Bedfordshire, where he continued to breed from many of the mares descended from the original Cliveden. From Hatley he produced St Leger winner Provoke (1965), a victory which earned Jakie more prize money (£42,431) than his father did altogether in either of his owners' winning years, 1925 (£37,723) and 1936 (£38,131).

But by 1973, Jakie Astor's proceeds from selling Sharp Edge were below the £30,000 it would now take an owner to run a string of fifty horses for a year. The sale finally dissolved a stud carefully built up ont he very best lines with the very best trainers.

One of the first Lord Astor's great rivals was the 17th Lord Derby, grandfather of the present lord, and, in his pomp, the most popular and widely-followed owner on the English turf. He had some of the greatest mares in racing history: Scapa Flow, Selene, Keystone, Canterbury Pilgrim, and the great stallion Hyperion who won the Derby in 1933. Between the wars, his Stanley Studs were the most powerful influence on the Thoroughbred anywhere in the world, an influence now the backbone of American breeding.

Unhappily, the present Earl sold almost all the valuable blood at Stanley House to pay death duties. These included many Hyperion mares which should not have left Britain; naturally, eager Americans gobbled them up.

Lord Rosebery was another regular breeder of high class horses which combined speed with stamina. Founded in 1840, his stud has produced six Derby winners, including Blue Peter (1939) and Ocean Swell (wartime 1944). This is another stud likely to vanish. All the stock has been sold and the two studs at Mentmore went up for sale following Lord Rosebery's death in 1974.

Tattersalls, one of Britain's three great salesrings for yearlings, is threatened by the strength of the thoroughbred scene in both Ireland and France.

The Homestall Stud at East Grinstead, owned by Lord Dewar and later by his son John, produced among others, Tudor Minstrel (the fastest horse Gordon Richards ever rode), Fair Trial and Commotion. Mated to Hyperion, Commotion produced Aristophanes. At first a moderate horse, he made such progress as a four-year-old he ended up carrying 9st 10lbs and beating horses giving him lumps of weight in the Hunt Cup. Exported to Argentina, Aristophanes sired Forli, the sire of Thatch, Home Guard and many other fine horses both there and in the United States. But, alas, grandeur and great success now seem to be things of the past for the Homestall Stud.

During World War I, two of the most famous and notorious owners in England were the Joel brothers, Solly and Jack. Stories about their exploits and their extravagant bids to outwit each other are numerous, scandalous and highly entertaining. In 1887 Jack Joel founded the Childwick Bury Stud near St Albans (run since 1940 by his son Jim). Solly Joel took over the Moulton Stud, Newmarket, from its founder Sir Ernest Cassel.

Winners bred at Childwick Bury included Sunstar (Two Thousand Guineas and Derby), Humourist (Derby), Princess Dorrie (One Thousand Guineas and The Oaks), Jest (One Thousand Guineas and The Oaks), and Royal Palace (Two Thousand Guineas and Derby). Jim Joel's best horse by far has been Royal Palace. Apart from his two Classic successes, he won the Eclipse Stakes, the Coronation Cup, King George VI Stakes, Prince of Wales Stakes and was unbeaten in five races as a four-year-old, altogether earning £166,063 in prize money. Yet this fine winner, with a first-class female line, has proved disappointing at stud to date. However, 1975 was his best year in England and France, suggesting an imminent revival. In 1976, as a twelve-year-old, he was represented on the course by his fifth crop.

The Dalham Hall Stud at Newmarket was founded in 1928 by the late Lord Milford to stand Flamingo, his Two Thousand Guineas winner of that year. The stud, now run by his son, the Honourable J. P. Phillips, is one of the most financially sound in Britain. In 1975 it broke all English records when their yearling colt by Mill Reef out of Lalibela made 202,000 guineas at Newmarket's Houghton sales. Grand Nephew, sire of Grundy, and Champion Sire of 1975, stands there. At Newmarket October sales and Houghton, they invariably receive top prices for their produce.

The Brook Stud at Chevaley, Newmarket, was laid out in 1927 and purchased by Sir Alfred Butt in the early 1930s. The stud, now run by Sir Alfred's son, Kenneth, maintains a very high standard of mare and topped the aggregate at the Newmarket October sales in 1959, 1968 and 1970, enabling them to graduate to Houghton. Selling there for the first time in 1972, they averaged 11,760 guineas and, in 1975, sold five yearlings for 44,400 guineas. Sir Kenneth Butt buys the occasional filly, e.g. Jacinth in 1971; she became best filly of her year and is now in the stud. Sir Kenneth said early in 1976 he had his best-ever collection of mares and he hoped to continue for a year or two to resist further fantastic offers for Jacinth, Shebeen, Galcia, Pristina and her daughter Princess Tina. Only studs run along the very best lines could afford to turn down such offers. In the long run, Brook Stud should benefit because they may be the only one left in England with any valuable foundation stock. The resident stallion is Amber Rama, whose first crop in 1972 made the remarkable average of 14,750 guineas.

The Royal Studs combine Hampton Court Stud, founded by Henry VIII, and Sandringham and Wolferton Studs, founded by Edward VII. Their outstanding breeding records embrace such winners as Sainfoin (Derby), Memoir (Oaks and St Leger), La Flèche (One Thousand Guineas, Oaks and St Leger), Persimmon (Derby and St Leger, Eclipse Stakes and Ascot Gold Cup), and Diamond Jubilee (Derby, Two Thousand Guineas, St Leger, Eclipse Stakes). Bustino took up stud duties at Wolferton in 1976 and another St Leger winner, Ribero, was then at the neighbouring Sandringham. The Queen's most recent Classic winner, the filly Highclere, in quick succession won the English One Thousand Guineas and the French Oaks, her Majesty's first Classic victory in France.

Robert Boucher sold the Sandwich Stud, Newmarket, in 1958 to the late Major L. B. Holliday and transferred his mares to his home in Kent where he built up the Norton Court Stud. Mr Boucher is famous for his colt Wilwyn, first-ever winner of the Washington International at Laurel, Maryland. The stud turns out a number of high-class yearlings, with top price to date of 26,000 guineas. His yearlings reached a high average. They bred Realm, an admirable sprinter who became leading first-season sire in 1975. This son of Princely Gift could well develop into one of the best sprinting sires.

The Swettenham Stud, near Macclesfield, Cheshire, was founded by Robert Sangster in 1968 to produce foals for the December sales. In 1972, seven foals averaged more than £10,000 each. Since then Robert Sangster has blossomed into an international stud owner with interests in Ireland, America and Australia.

The Burton Agnes Stud, near Driffield, Yorkshire, is another long-established commercial stud selling impressive yearlings, whose top price so far is 41,000 guineas for a colt by So Blessed out of Borona. The Pinfold Stud, near Market Drayton in Shropshire, bred Pieces of Eight and Petingo, among other winners, and has obtained a top yearling price of 31,000 guineas. The late William Hill, the bookmaker, founded Whitsbury Manor Stud in 1943 and two years later bought Sezincote Stud. Breeding the best yearlings and standing some outstanding sires, they topped Newmarket sales in 1973, obtaining 55,000 guineas for an Amber Rama–Jaffa filly.

So many fine horses have been produced, yet British breeders must now cast envious eyes across the Irish Sea, English Channel and the Atlantic to note horse racing keyed to incentives, prosperity and sure survival.

14 SUCCESS SMELLS EVEN SWEETER THAN THE BLUE GRASS

Richard Baerlein

American stud farms are horse empires, very different from European studs. Since World War II, thoroughbred production has become a multi-billion dollar industry, with 50,000 active racehorses representing 6,000 sires.

Their breeders have shrewdly bought the best overseas sires, including the late Aga Khan's three Derby winners, Blenheim, Mahmoud and Bahram before the war and Tulyar just after peace returned. More vitally, they bought Nasrullah, bred and raced by the Aga Khan, from Irishman Joseph McGrath, who had acquired him from the Aga. They opened their wallets wide to import Vaguely Noble and Seabird and to lease Ribot, unbeaten winner of sixteen races, for his entire lifetime at stud. In, too, came the best brood mares from Europe and almost all the Hyperion mares from England.

In 1972, at Claiborne Stud in Paris, Kentucky, I calculated the stallions in one barn alone would fetch more than £20 million. One passed quickly from Nijinsky to Sir Ivor, to Forli, to Buckpasser, to Round Table, to Secretariat, to Riva Ridge and on to a dozen other superb stallions from all parts of the world. Even in the off-season, when all visiting mares have left Claiborne, some 300 mares are there as permanent boarders. More battalions of champion stallions confront you at other great studs: thirty-five at Mr Leslie Combs's Spendthrift Farms in Lexington, Kentucky; twenty-two at Gainesway Farms, also in Lexington; stablesfull at Edward P. Taylor's two establishments – Winfields Farms in Toronto and Chesapeake City, Maryland.

All are thriving, efficient business complexes completely beyond the comprehension of any foreign blood stock fancier who has never visited one. But their scope and vision are being emulated elsewhere, most notably in Eire by Robert Sangster, John Magnier and partners at Coolmore and Castle Hyde stud farms, and at Tim Rogers' Airlie stud at Lucan, Co. Meath.

The Americans leave nothing to chance. The biggest studs run their own veterinary laboratories controlled by outstandingly-qualified staff; they

The time the place and the age of promise: springtime in Lexington, Kentucky, where there is the greatest, and most expensive, concentration of thoroughbred horses in the world. *Photo: Courtesy of Planned Public Relations International Ltd.*

make up their own food (invariably some form of nuts); they keep the minutest records of every resident horse. All this helps them to reap the finest rewards: American studs produced four Epsom Derby winners in five years – Sir Ivor, 1968; Nijinsky, 1970; Mill Reef, 1971; and Roberto, 1972.

After the English-bred Vaguely Noble had won the 1968 Arc de Triomphe, defeating Sir Ivor by three lengths, he was syndicated for $5,000,000, a sum considered untoppable. In fact, it was twice equalled before a syndicate paid $190,000 for each of thirty-two shares (totalling $6,080,000) to buy Secretariat. Then, in autumn 1975, this record vanished when three-year-old Wajima (like Secretariat, a son of Bold Ruler–Nasrullah), was syndicated for $7,200,000. As a yearling, Wajima had cost $600,000, almost double the 136,000 guineas paid for Vaguely Noble after he had won the Observer Gold Cup at Doncaster by seven lengths.

The influence of Nearco blood on American thoroughbreds has been one of the greatest stories in turf history. Yet, as recently as 1949, the only branch of the Phalaris (grand sire of Nearco) family standing in America was Rustom Sirdar. That year, the late A. B. (Bull) Hancock, jnr, triggered off the historic impetus. He bought Nasrullah, Nearco's son, who had a season at Claiborne Farm before being sent for a time to England, where he was leading sire in 1951.

For Europeans, Claiborne, now run by Bull's son Seth, is unquestionably America's most famous stud, and Bull Hancock, the supreme artist at spotting stallions of great potential, was perhaps the most famous racing expert of all. When he died in 1972 he had in the previous twenty years bred winners of more than $19,000,000. For fifteen years in a row the leading American sire was a Claiborne stallion; Nasrullah and his son, Bold Ruler, earned twelve of these titles. For six of these years the runner-up was also from Claiborne. One year it produced all three top stallions. His son, Seth, now runs Claiborne and will undoubtedly keep it at the very top.

Another great stud, Spendthrift, was named for the progenitor of one of the best and most lasting male lines in America.

Spendthrift, foaled in 1876, was a great racehorse, the sire of Hastings, who in turn sired Fair Play, the sire of the immortal Man O'War. The 2,800-acre stud was founded by Leslie Combs, great grandfather of the present manager. The founder's grandson, known to all as Mr Spendthrift, retired in 1975 in favour of his son Brownell. More than 200 mares are permanently stationed there, and Never Bend, sire of Mill Reef, is certainly the best known to European racegoers of its thirty-eight stallions.

Brilliant success, too, embellishes the history of Mr John Gaines's Gainesway Farm. Noted American owner, Mr Nelson Bunker-Hunt, sent Vaguely Noble there after, in 1968, gaining control of the horse: when Vaguely Noble was syndicated for $5,000,000, Bunker-Hunt's twenty-eight shares made him the largest single shareholder.

Nijinsky, (Lester Piggott) comfortably winning the 1970 St. Leger, the year he also won the Derby. The champion horse later went to stand at Claiborne, finest of American stud farms.

Vaguely Noble's first crop of three-year-olds made him leading European sire of 1973; he won the title again in 1974 with the brilliant Dahlia as his chief earner. Dahlia won the Eclipse Award – the stud world's 'Oscar' – for champion turf horse, three-year-old and upwards. Also in 1974 another Gainesway stallion, Bold Bidder, was a world-leading sire. Vaguely Noble's blood is so strongly represented at Gainesway (his sons Ace of Aces, Gunter, Mississippian and Noble Decree all stand there), that he could prove a good out-cross for Nasrullah and Nearco stallions which are beginning to over-populate some American studs.

Perhaps the most towering figure of the American turf is Edward Plunkett-Taylor, now in his mid-seventies. In 1970 when Nijinsky, whom he bred, won the Triple Crown in England, Taylor became the world's number one breeder: produce of his studs won $1,069,553 in North America, $564,582 in England and Ireland, $86,400 in France – a grand total of $1,720,535

That summer he became the first man to breed both Kentucky Derby (Northern Dancer) and Epsom Derby (Nijinsky) winners. In August 1970 the nine-year-old Northern Dancer was syndicated for $2,400,000 and, within forty-eight hours, Nijinsky was syndicated for $5,440,000.

Eddie Taylor is the architect of modern racing in Canada, having begun with Windfields stud on the outskirts of Toronto. (Windfields, foaled in 1943, was the first stake winner he had bred.) After the original stud was converted into a housing estate, Taylor bought the National Stud at Oshawa, twenty miles outside Toronto, and in 1968 bought a stud at Chesa-peake City, Maryland, which is becoming one of the most imposing studs in America – Northern Dancer was sent there.

His great success began at the Newmarket December sales in 1952, when he bought (for 10,500 guineas) the Hyperion mare Lady Angela, then in foal to Nearco. His stipulation for purchasing her was that she drop her foal in England and be covered again by Nearco before crossing the Atlantic. It proved a momentous decision.

Her first foal was an unprepossessing chestnut with a wretched pair of hocks. Lady Angela was covered again and, when certified with foal, was shipped to Canada. This foal, Nearctic, revolutionised breeding in North America: he sired Northern Dancer, who in turn sired Nijinsky. In 1967 Taylor syndicated Nearctic for $1,050,000, still a record for a thirteen-year-old sire. Taylor knows there is a danger his stud may get too much Nearco blood, just as Bunker-Hunt will one day have concern with Vaguely Noble.

'I am all the time looking for some complete out-cross,' says Taylor, explaining why he bought English Derby winner Snow Night. Taylor began a sales system which I believe is unique. He pre-prices yearlings on his farm twenty-four hours before inspection. Then the buyers come along. Horses which fail to find buyers at the right price are put into training. The system has been lucky: no buyer would give the asking price of $35,000 for Nearctic, nor the $25,000 for Northern Dancer. Of course Taylor lost others which became valuable, but nothing he bred until Nijinsky ever really equalled these two horses, either on the track or at stud.

In 1971 Taylor began selling at Saratoga and here the opening offer was for the reserve. For the buyer it is a far quicker and more satisfactory method of selling than in England, where the reserve is hidden from buyers and sometimes takes several minutes to be reached.

Northern Dancer was put in with such a low reserve of $25,000 for three-fold reasons: he was the first foal of both his sire and dam; he was very late (from a June 28 mating) and he was a tiny foal of only 14h 2½in.

Quality abounds. Success smells even sweeter than the blue grass. The money, organisation and magnificent blood lines in America are truly awesome.

15 THE BATTLE OF BEERSHEBA

Murray Hedgcock

The First World War started with the horse: it ended with the tank.

Cavalrymen believed in 1914 that this conflict would offer them a decisive role. Instead it marked the twilight of the mounted soldier. It was not arthritic decline; part of the late afternoon sky was shot through with gleaming colours. The richest of these belonged to one mounted force which had a mere three years as a horse-equipped fighting group in action; it became immortal through one of the epic cavalry charges of all wars.

The Australian Light Horse, mounted riflemen drawn from the infant Commonwealth States, over-ran massed, dug-in Turkish defences at Beersheba, Palestine, on October 31, 1917. This charge, with the westering sun almost touching the sand dunes, was, for one solid reason, more memorable than that of the Light Brigade: it was glorious success against the Light Brigade's 'glorious' failure; the Light Horse, too, bred no General Custer. So, in the midst of the reds, blues and golds of primped hussars and dragoons taking history's salute jogs the recklessly brave light horseman drably dressed except for his rakish emu-plumed slouch hat.

Raffish and independently-minded, these citizen soldiers ruffled the mightiest feathers; Allenby's for instance. General Sir Edmund Allenby, British C-I-C- Palestine, assailed the rowdyism and cussedness of Australian troops. But, at the end of the war, he wrote about them in Palestine: 'The Australian light horseman combines with a splendid physique a restless activity of mind. This mental quality renders him somewhat impatient of rigid and formal discipline, but it confers upon him the gift of adaptability, and this is the secret of much of his success, mounted or on foot.

'In this dual role, on every variety of ground – mountain, plain, desert, swamp or jungle – the Australian light horseman has proved himself equal to the best.'

The finest combination in Australian military history: a fully-equipped light horse trooper on his Waler horse in Palestine during World War I, *Photo: Courtesy Australian War Memorial.*

The enemy, with gills greener than a Killarney landscape, also acknowledged him. In May 1918 the Turkish radio declared: 'Es Salt has been captured by the reckless and dashing gallantry of the Australian cavalry.' A German staff officer present at this attack on the Turkish Fourth Army H.Q. said men of the Eighth Light Horse Regiment had galloped their horses in places where no-one else would have ridden at all.

This unsolicited testimonial was almost a reprise of two lines about a horseman from a famous Australian poem *The Man from Snowy River*:
'Few could ride beside him when his blood was fairly up,
For he could go wherever horse and man could go.'
As we shall see, both men and horses of this renowned regiment were outstandingly different from all others united to commit carnage.

The Australian Light Horse had roots in the withdrawal from the Australian colonies of imperial troops in 1870, when the colonials realized they were alone, undefended, 10,000 miles from mother England. Local all-volunteer mounted forces did exist, but the country needed a regular defence.

Each colony developed its existing forces: in the original settlement, the Royal New South Wales Lancers was the major mounted force. Elsewhere each colonial government organized local and highly individual volunteer troops – such as the Castlemaine Dragoons – under the less flamboyant title of 'mounted rifles'.

First action for the eager new commands came with the Boer War. A total of 838 officers, 15,327 other ranks and 16,314 horses sailed to South Africa where they fought bravely and well, gaining experience that hundreds were to find invaluable when they returned to the colours a dozen years later for a world war.

In 1905 the Australian Commonwealth government established eighteen light horse regiments: One and Five Brigades drawn from New South Wales; Three and Four from Victoria; plus regiments from Queensland, South Australia and Western Australia. By the time World War I broke out the Australian Light Horse was the mounted arm of the country's army: twenty-three regiments had a total of 456 officers and 6,508 other ranks.

The light horseman rode a Waler – an ungainly name derived simply, and dully, from New South Wales. The typical Waler was the progeny of thoroughbred stallions bought fairly cheap in Britain and shipped to Australia to service local mares. Their offspring normally were rather light but extremely tough: Australia was mostly free from animal diseases and most owners could handle any needed doctoring. Usually left outdoors the year round, the Waler's simple, hardening life made him so well suited to the rigours of the desert campaign where the half-bred weight-carrying hunters of British regiments struggled. Before Palestine, the Walers had proved themselves in India, in the Russo–Japanese wars – the Japanese were eager buyers – and especially in South Africa, often owner-ridden.

The horses had to be resolute. They carried twenty or twenty-one stones in weight – rider and equipment – but responded bravely and perkily even when cut to half normal rations or forced to go without water for thirty-six hours – and longer.

In 1914 the Army stated in its aridly precise way that the light horse rider carried 39 pounds $8\frac{1}{4}$ ounces of gear, ranging from puttees to bandolier with one-hundred rounds of ·303 ammunition. A further 76 pounds $5\frac{1}{4}$ ounces weight was distributed about the horse, including the rider's greatcoat, wallets containing one pair of spare socks, boot laces and sundry items, and (the most vital) hoofpicker implement.

Ordnance wizards quoted the rider's weight at 140 pounds. This nonsense betrayed the savagery of demands made on the Australian horses: how many troopers weighed no more than ten stones?

A twelve-stone trooper carrying regulation equipment was burdening his horse with just over twenty stone weight. And this in the Sinai desert in 1916–18 baked by centuries of heat, lashed by fierce winds and often shifting sand for a foot-hold.

Standard procedure was a forty-minute ride, then a ten-minute spell with rider leading horse, then a ten-minute break for both. Watering inevitably was a major problem, especially after assured water supplies of base camp were left behind and the trek across Sinai began. After early experiments, the original three waterings were cut back to two; the horses fared equally well. This saved water and could save time if watering meant diverging up to half-a-dozen miles to well or stream.

Toting the horses' food supplies was another logistical worry: a rider's daily ration weighed two or three pounds; a horse's twenty very bulky pounds.

In theory horses need five gallons of water a day. Often these Walers got half this, or less. Once or twice they endured heroically for as long as seventy hours without watering, while their riders too – officially getting one gallon a day – often were cut to a quart, and at times even to a pint. And all too often desert wells or pools proved so nauseous that horses refused to drink and men who eagerly filled water-bottles vomited at first gulp.

Who were the Light Horsemen themselves? Basically they were Australia's countrymen: towns and cities had filled most of the infantry ranks.

In this vast young land the horse was then a vital creature; it was natural that mounted units tapped large numbers of rural men knowing nothing about uniforms and warfare but much about horses. Many who wore the plumed hats were pioneers or sons of pioneers who had volunteered after recruiting began in 1914, bringing their own cherished horses they had bought or bred and schooled.

The war history records the range of recruits: 'They represented every phase of Australia's diverse rural industries: dairymen and small cultivators from the long rich coastal belt between the Dividing Range and the sea: orchardists from the foothills; timber-getters from sparkling forests on the ranges; men from the larger farms of the long wheat-belt, on the inside slope of the mountains; and men whose lives had been spent on the sheep and cattle stations of the vast inland plains.'

Brought up in a hot, dry land, the light horseman knew the urgency of conserving water, of doing everything to minimise effects of the Middle East's furnace heat. They fitted into such testing conditions far more readily than did British yeomanry regiments, fresh from the temperate British Isles.

Horsemanship was high. To be sure the flow of light horse recruits, heavy from the outset, had contained many non-riders (including a glass-eyed scallawag who actually passed the medical) anxious to avoid the infantry-man's foot-slogging lot. They were weeded – and many literally thrown – out, hurtling from their horses when they tried their non-existent skills.

Once mustered into the ranks, the recruit could don the distinctive head-gear of the light horseman: the digger slouch hat with plumes at the emblem of the mounted soldier. Originally the New South Wales Light Horse had worn black cocks' plumes; the Victorians a single emu feather; the West Australians a black swan feather and riders from Queensland, South Australia and Tasmania a group of emu feathers. After 1914, emu feathers cluster became the common badge.

Light horsemen showed their disdain for regulations by seldom, or never, wearing their uniforms complete or according to regulations. To the bafflement of proper British officers, they tossed aside tunics, shirts, singlets and assembled their entire uniforms from whatever garments they saw fit or had left. Photographs of Light Horse units show a jumble of styles: officers in shirts ranging from chocolate brown to off-white; footwear from high what-ho riding boots to ankle boots worn with leggings or puttees; multi-hued breeches from Sandhurst proper flaring to lion-tamer dramatic.

Uneasiness stirred in the breasts of British brass who lived by rules and rectitude whenever a single light horse trooper or group cantered by. The sartorial exuberance, the dangling hand-rolled cigarette, the slouch hat sometimes pinned up at the left-side, sometimes the right: all truly reflected the casual, bull-hating insouciance of these non-professional soldiers.

'Not only do your men fail to salute me when I ride through your camp, but they laugh out loud at my orderlies,' exploded indignant Lieutenant-General Sir Philip Chetwode after he took command of Desert Column, a unified force that linked the Allied mounted forces in early stages of the Sinai campaign. Eventually the Australians' easy discipline and the tight organisation of British troops did reach a sort of accommodation. But Australian forces always resented not having direct contact with their own government; they were always somewhat at the mercy of the War Office in London; English rather than Australian officers were given many key posts.

While the Light Horse officers corps did contain big landowners and variegated professional men, even they were not gentlemen in the English tradition. This democracy was a source of strength: it helped give the force its quality. For, despite some loutishness revealed in overdrinking and larrikinism on leave, the troopers behaved themselves in a fashion that occupying armies have rarely matched.

The first Australian light horsemen had sailed from the Western Australian port of Albany on October 25, 1914, their ranks comfortably sprinkled with South African veterans amid pathetically eager youngsters, many of whom were on their first journey beyond native shores.

Early plans were for them to go to England to train there for fighting in France, which the British High Command considered the major theatre of war. Fortunately for the light horsemen their liaison officers reported conditions in Britain were so unsuitable the Australians were switched to base camps in Cairo. At this time the British military role in the Middle East was uncertain: broadly they planned to defend the Suez Canal if any assault were made on it, and not much more.

After the first Gallipoli landings in 1915, the war chiefs decided to throw some of the light horse – all volunteers – into that ill-fated expedition. The men went dismounted: horses could do nothing in the fearful conditions. Many troopers were killed before the survivors were withdrawn and able to return to the mounted role they knew. After the rigours of Gallipoli, the mud and the filth, the shock of trench warfare and the trauma of seeing mates shot to pieces alongside them, the Light Horsemen regained strength and enthusiasm in the warmth and calm of Egypt.

On January 10, 1916, an experienced British officer, General Sir Archibald Murray, took over as commander of the Eastern Expeditionary Force. Sixteen days later the Anzac Mounted Division was formally set up, to be commanded from March 16 by its almost legendary leader, Major-General Sir Harry Chauvel.

Chauvel has been called the greatest leader of horse in modern times. Born in 1865 on the cattle station at Clarence River, New South Wales, owned by his retired Indian army officer grandfather, Chauvel had grown up with horses. He made a local reputation as an amateur rider at picnic race meetings, noted for his cool control of himself and his mount. When Australian volunteers went to South Africa, Chauvel joined the Queensland Mounted Infantry. Later he led a composite force of Australian, Canadian, British and South African horsemen.

At the outbreak of World War I, he was on his way to Britain to serve as Australian representative on the Imperial General Staff at the War Office. On arrival he was promptly diverted to command the mounted force being assembled in Egypt. Chauvel, who was promoted to brigadier after serving at Gallipoli, was an unlikely man to head the lively, irreverent, tough-talking

Australian troops. He was small and wiry; he was reserved, even aloof in manner, quiet and gentle in speech; a very shy person who could never pretend to be one of the boys. But he proved himself a leader of strength and purpose who planned his campaigns carefully. If he never earned hero-worship, he had the respect of his men. His peculiar skill was to get full value from the mobility and flexibility of his mounted horsemen. The Light Horse was generally outnumbered when directly facing their enemy in Sinai and Palestine. Careful disposition of his men showed Chauvel's quality and it brought him the very best results. The Anzac Mounted Division consisted of three Light Horse Brigades plus the New Zealand Mounted Rifles Brigade; later Chauvel was to command the Desert Mounted Corps comprising, as well as Anzacs, British yeomanry and Indian cavalry. But his name glows in history as leader of the Australian Light Horse.

Lieutenant General Sir Harry Chauvel, G.O.C., Desert Mounted Corps, (*far left*) leading his troops through Damascus after they had captured it for the Allies.
Photo: Courtesy Australian War Memorial.

As mentioned earlier, the centrepiece of their – and Chauvel's – glory was the winning of Beersheba, an exploit forged from the instinctive gallantry of which truly great military triumphs are made.

In June, 1917, when Allenby became commander of the British Army in Palestine, he flung himself into the task of routing the Turkish and German forces, which to that point had recorded some successes against the British. His immediate aim was to break the Gaza–Beersheba line, running from the Mediterranean port of Gaza inland about thirty miles to the town of Beersheba. Then he hoped to sweep through Palestine and capture Jerusalem before the enemy could regroup in the wake of a massive reorganisation and strengthening of the British forces.

Tactically, the Gaza–Beersheba break had to be made with cobra-striking speed. So it proved. When the Light Horse did attack Beersheba on October 31, barely an hour's daylight remained. The advancing troopers were still four miles from enemy trenches defending the town. Chauvel, commander of the Desert Mounted Corps, discussed the prospect with Brigadier-General William Grant, commander of Four Light Horse Brigade – a Queensland pastoralist described by the official war historian as 'somewhat more impulsive and excitable than most of the light horse leaders.'

Grant urged: 'Give me a free hand and my brigade will take the town.' Asked how he proposed to do this, he explained, 'By an open cavalry charge, Sir.'

Chauvel, under orders from Allenby to capture Beersheba by nightfall, gave permission. The lean, wiry figure of Grant dashed away to instruct his brigade officers. The Fourth (Victorian) Regiment, under Lieutenant-Colonel M. W. J. Bourchier, a Strethmerton grazier, and the Twelfth (New South Wales), under Lieutenant-Colonel D. Cameron, also a grazier, of Scone district, had not expected combat that day.

They had spent a quiet few hours in rest: when they received the order to charge, they were delighted – this was stuff to excite a mounted soldier's heart.

It is important to remember that, technically, the Light Horse was not a cavalry force, but mounted infantry whose basic weapon was the rifle. Riders did not use sword or lance, though late in the desert campaign – after Beersheba – some did have swords issued to them. Their basic weapons were rifle and bayonet; for cavalry-style advantage they rode with bayonets in hand. Protecting them from the rear were machine-gun squadrons.

Now the light horsemen drew up in squadron frontage, in three lines, three-hundred to five-hundred yards apart, with four-to-five paces separating each trooper. They set off at a trot. But only briefly. The need for speed and surprise quickly propelled them to the gallop. Opening bursts of shrapnel and then machine-gun fire blasted a few troopers from their saddles, but did not slow the advance; their blood was up.

As they rushed nearer, rifle fire from Turkish trenches brought down many horses in the leading line. But enemy fire grew wilder and looser. The astounded and petrified Turks discovered these horsemen were coming all the way bellowing madly and waving their weapons. Forgetting to adjust their sights the entrenched soldiers poured most of their shots far above the horsemen's heads.

Still the Australians charged on. Their horses soared over the first trench – shallow and uncompleted, with only a handful of riflemen defending it – and the Light Horse swept on to the main line close behind it. This line was in places ten feet deep and four feet wide, heavily defended. Major J. Lawson, a Yorkshireman who had migrated to Australia to run a hotel in the Victorian Wimmera farming town of Rupanyup, sped his leading squadron over the line and into a nest of tents and dugouts where the horsemen leapt down to rush the enemy with their bayonets. They cut down thirty or forty Turks in this hand-to-hand fighting before the survivors · threw down their rifles and surrendered.

Australian horsemen petrified the Turks during their encounters at Es Salt in Palestine. Among the casualties were these Australian pack horses who died at the entrance to the town. *Photo: Courtesy Australian War Memorial.*

On the left flank, the 12th Regiment, led by Major E. M. Hyman, a farmer from Tamworth, New South Wales, charged over the trenches. As Hyman and a mere dozen men dismounted to clean up the demoralised defenders, the bulk of his command hurtled through a gap in the lines – and galloped straight into Beersheba.

Captain R. K. Robey, an estate manager from the Clarence River, New South Wales, led the rush into the town, while another group, led by a Scone grazier, Captain J. R. C. Davies, careered down the main street. Beersheba was in chaos: its bewildered defenders were fleeing pellmell from the British advance. Having watched the earlier fighting, they had confidently anticipated holding the town until reinforcements arrived. Now Turks were scrambling out towards the hills to the north and north-west. They limbered up artillery pieces and hastily clattered out of town; engineers who had prepared demolition charges against abandoning Beersheba simply fled with the job unfinished.

The Australians continued rampaging through the town and out in pursuit of fugitives until intensifying fire from the Turkish stronghold in the hills – and the whiff of assured victory – turned them back. Scattered fighting still seethed in side streets. Small pockets of isolated defenders fired a few buildings and blew up railway points. But soon after nightfall the entire town was in Australian hands and prisoners were under guard.

At 11 p.m., when General Grant and his staff rode into Beersheba, the men and horses who had made this astonishing charge could finally drink, eat, relax and sleep.

Extraordinary instances of achievement abounded, some of them typical of the 'larrakin' spirit, in the best sense of the word, that imbued these Australians. Trooper T. O'Leary, a stationhand from Maryborough, Queensland, now a ground scout, was probably first man into Beersheba township, charging almost one-hundred yards ahead of the squadron – and then disappearing. Ninety minutes later, with the town captured, he was found in a side street sitting on a field piece with six Turkish soldiers meekly holding his horse. O'Leary explained he had captured the gun single-handed and made the Turks drive it away so no other regiment could claim it as a trophy. The officer who found him was from his regiment, so the trophy was saved, and O'Leary won the Military Medal.

Armourer Staff-Sergeant A. J. Cox, an assayer from the Bendigo gold-fields, found a Turkish crew setting up a machine-gun from a mule as the first Australians were dismounted and dashing into the trenches. Before it could be set up – and at close quarters it would have taken heavy toll – Cox rushed the crew, disarmed them and took forty prisoners single-handed. Cox won the Distinguished Conduct Medal.

Mounted stretcher-bearers rode forward as usual with the advance line and aided the wounded as fighting threshed around the trenches. One bearer was Private Albert Cotter, a Glebe (Sydney) clerk best known as one of Australia's most feared fast bowlers who had played twenty-one tests for Australia. Cotter had been singled out at the second Gaza battle for fine work under heavy fire: 'He behaved in action as a man without fear,' the war history stated. Sadly at Beersheba, working among dismounted combatants, and a few weeks short of his thirty-fourth birthday, Cotter was shot dead at close range.

Facing:
Photographed here in Colorado, this magnificent pure-bred Arabian stallion The Shah was imported into England by Major and Mrs. T. W. I. Hedley.

Over page:
Mill Reef, one of the greatest race horses ever and winner of the Derby 1971.

The Queen on Betsy at Windsor.

Light horse casualties, however, were amazingly light: thirty-two officers and men were killed, thirty-two wounded – most of the casualties coming not in the charge but in the trench fighting. For this cost, the horsemen had captured a town, thirty-eight officers and seven-hundred other ranks (as well as killing about one-hundred Turks), nine field guns, three machine-guns and much other materials. This instantly-famous charged showed that determined horsemen could over-run defenders dug into fairly strong positions: it swept the British advance to a launching-point for the offensive that was to lead to the triumphal entry into Jerusalem just thirty-nine days later.

It helped crush the confidence of the Turkish army. Their commander reported to his headquarters in an intercepted wireless message that his troops had broken because they were 'terrified of the Australian cavalry.' The Turks never forgot Beersheba. Their own cavalry had always been wary of the Australian Light Horse – bigger, stronger men on bigger, stronger, faster horses – and their infantry now faced increasingly the prospect of being ridden down by the Australians, British yeomanry, Indian lancers or French chasseurs.

General Allenby disliked the insouciance of Light Horsemen but admired their courage. Here, he has just presented the Military Medal to S.Q.M.S.D. Michael of the First Australian Light Horse, while two officers have a quiet natter amongst themselves.
Photo: Courtesy Australian War Memorial.

One tantalising souvenir was the most famous photograph of the actual charge. Controversy swirled around this photograph for decades: sceptics argued that an authentic head-on shot of this short-notice action had been impossible, A half century later, in 1967, the photographer, Mr Eric Elliott, of the Melbourne suburb of Moorabbin, signed an affidavit that he had been ahead of the Australian troops preparing maps as a range-finder with a small unit ready for an anticipated attack the next day (November 1, 1917). To his amazement he found himself directly in the line of gallop. He took his photograph, then spurred his horse away for his life, or he would have been run down.

Throughout the war, the Light Horse had galloped alongside British Army mounted and infantry regiments, Indian lancers, French North African chasseurs and Spahis. And with their New Zealand mates never far away, they surged through Palestine as Allenby steadily advanced throughout 1917. On December 9, 1917, the Tenth Light Horse from Western Australia were the first mounted troops into Jerusalem, their sturdy walers startling the inhabitants used to compact slender Arab ponies.

Allied forces moved steadily across Palestine until, on September 19, Allenby launched the final attack that was to capture Damascus, the last Turkish stronghold. On September 30, Major L. C. Timperley, of Geraldton, Western Australia, and Major A. C. N. Olden, in civilian life a dentist, led their squadron into the city. At 6.30 a.m. they rode up to the town hall, revolvers in hand, and accepted the surrender of the civic authorities.

Exactly one month later, the Turkish government signed an armistice with the Western Powers, and on November 11, the armistice with Germany was signed. But the Light Horse was not finished with Middle East action: before they returned home they helped put down a brief, ragged uprising in Egypt. By August 1919 the Australian Light Horse was home again. The rundown of the fighting force was under way; survivors of those cheerful volunteers of almost five years earlier were civilians again. Afterwards the romance of armed man on horseback was a casualty of history; the diesel motor snuffed out the Light Horse and every cavalry corps.

Today, seventy years after the Light Horse came into being, its memory survives proudly and vibrantly. The name exists, too: the 4/19 Prince of Wales Light Horse is based at Bougainville Barracks in Carlton, Victoria. Its 'A' Squadron is based at Sale, the Gippsland town where once they rode in to join the original unit: timber-cutters from Heyfield, dairy farmers from Maffra, stockmen from the Dargo High Plains, small holders from out towards Ninety Mile Beach.

Modern warfare is a crueller aberration than ever. But gallantry cannot be demeaned. So the name of Australian Light Horse will always shine with the gleam of an unsheathed bayonet catching the fierce desert sunlight.

16 ROYAL HORSES

Judith Campbell

For centuries horses were one of the important symbols of the might of the Crown, the Monarch's courser of state a tangible emblem of royal power and prestige. Ceremonial animals such as these were required to be big and impressive, with a high-stepping, 'showy' action and plenty of fire and 'presence', and it is likely that the Sovereign, sitting his richly caparisoned horse, was more concerned with its looks than with its personality. It was left to the royal knight at arms and his battle charger to develop the relationship of mutual trust and dependency, which so often exists between horseman and horse, that made King Richard II love his Roan Barbary 'like a son.'

As time passed kings ceased to lead their troops in battle, monarchs no longer made royal progressions on horseback to impress their subjects. The royal relationship with horses continued, but gradually changed in character. By the time Queen Victoria came to the throne horses were still providing transport for princes and peasants alike, but the royal riding horses were kept more for pleasure than prestige.

There are photographs of Lochnagar, or Fyvie, or one of the other Highland ponies that the Queen found so surefooted and good at 'scrambling up over stones and everything' during her explorations of the Scottish Highlands. But these depict them with the staid, middle-aged Queen, her habit of sobre black bombasine, the ghillie John Brown in control at the pony's head. At the beginning of her reign there was no photography to portray the horses that gave the young Victoria so much pleasure, in the days when she was often prone to gallop off in all directions.

In 1837 a horse called Leopold, 'very handsomely harnessed,' was the Queen's choice as charger for reviewing her troops in the Home Park at Windsor. She wore a dark blue velvet habit with red collar and cuffs, adorned with the blue, gold-edged garter ribbon, and must have made an

Princess Anne on Arthur of Troy, Chatsworth 1975.

Queen Victoria by
Landseer.

The Queen and Prince
Albert fording the Gary.

enchanting picture. But bearing in mind the sedate, obedient walk required today of any horse the Queen rides at the Trooping the Colour on Horseguards Parade, it seems surprising that her great-great-grandmother and her G.O.C. escort actually cantered to and from the lines of soldiers she was inspecting. When the performance was repeated the following year Leopold, a horse of spirit, increased his pace to the point where his royal rider, nonchalantly noting the fact in her diary, 'had thought he might be running away!'

In those years the young Queen undoubtedly enjoyed speed, and often led a cavalcade of thirty or more members of her court on a 'charming ride' that included a three-mile gallop. For these occasions she was usually mounted on her dear Tartar, a little dark-brown horse with a springy action and excellent manners. Often it was Monarch who carried the Queen when she was riding in Hyde Park with Lord Melbourne, her Prime Minister, discussing affairs of state. And this was the horse that shied violently one day to tip her off at the feet of her Prime Minister's horse – much to Lord Melbourne's consternation, and his young sovereign's amusement.

Nowadays the private riding horses kept in the royal mews at Windsor are a source of great pleasure to the Queen and her family and guests, and also provide most necessary relaxation. The Queen rides whenever she can spare the time, and has inherited her great-great-grandmother's liking for an occasional good gallop. In the days when Princess Anne and her pony High Jinks were getting the measure of each other, the Queen once led an unsuspecting contingent of her guests, regardless of their prowess as horsemen, in a merry spin over Anne's miniature cross-country course at Windsor.

This was in the era of Betsy, the black mare with more character than blue blood that was bought from a farmer in 1953 and remained the royal favourite until she was well into her twenties. A creature of feminine moods, usually gay and willing but occasionally sulky, Betsy in winter sometimes looked unbecomingly hirsute as she objected strongly to having her face and head clipped. When she was eventually retired, the Queen decided, rather to her Stud Manager's surprise, to breed from the mare. But Betsy, always one to make up her own mind, declined to have anything to do with the idea, and ended her days, a pampered, plebeian spinster, in the private paddocks alongside those inhabited by the thoroughbred aristocrats of the Queen's Hampton Court stud.

Unless the Queen has bred a horse herself, she often has little choice in her prospective riding horses. They tend to turn up at the Windsor mews either as gifts or as animals that have declined to fill the role allotted to them, or they are retired.

Sultan was a present from the President of Pakistan in 1959, a handsome thoroughbred of the same classical breeding as one given to the Shah of

Iran. He was a strong, rather impetuous ride with an endearing habit of squealing with joy when asked to gallop or jump; but the Queen was very fond of him and Sultan carried her well for many years. He belonged to the same period as Betsy, and also Pride, given by King Hussein of Jordan, that became a general favourite the moment he appeared, wearing a colourful and embroidered Bedouin headstall with tassells. In the early days the Queen frequently rode her little Arabian horse, and despite his tendency to sense 'dragons' lurking in the undergrowth, she thoroughly enjoyed Pride's *joie de vivre*; so did Princess Anne, who as a schoolgirl used him as her second string. Now retired, the little horse from Jordan is living out his days in the comforts of the Polhampton Stud, leased by the Queen, close by Hampton Court.

Bussaco completed the trio of gift horses of the fifties, presented by the President of Portugal. He was a sweet-natured, chestnut stallion of the Lusitano breed, and having been schooled on the same lines as a Portuguese rejoneador's horse, was always a most obedient and delightful ride. The Queen rode Bussaco occasionally, and he was very popular with her guests. He was then loaned to a stud and later for a while the Queen rode his son, the aptly named Oporto, out of Pampera, one of the Crown Equerry's polo mares. Eventually this horse was owned and ridden by the event rider, Debbie West, and until he unfortunately 'broke down', Oporto was showing potential as an event horse.

The three horses that the Queen rides most frequently today are very different types, but she finds them equally good companions whether riding in the park at Windsor or along the wooded tracks at Sandringham, galloping on the open Norfolk fields or wending her way amongst the heather on the hill at Balmoral.

In his earlier days Princess Anne's comment on Cossack, the eldest of the trio, was that he could sometimes be 'very Russian!' Now seventeen, this dun horse, out of Suete, one of Prince Philip's polo-pony mares, was sired by Zaman, a golden dun Karabakh, given to the Queen some years ago from the state stud in the Republic of Azerbaijan, where these small horses are bred chiefly for racing.

Bellboy, younger by two years, was bred by the Queen at Sandringham and is a half-brother to Columbus, the big grey ridden first by Princess Anne and then by Mark Phillips. Until he injured himself he was a distinct hope for the 1976 Olympic eventing team. But although they shared the same mother, the Queen's Trim Anne, Bellboy, sired by Le Belle, has missed out on the rough, tough character Columbus inherited from his father, Colonist II, and is a mannered, amenable ride.

To some extent the horse the Queen rides to the Trooping the Colour should be of the right stamp, and a good colour to show off the modified guard's uniform she wears, but temperament is the most important factor.

It has to remain unperturbed by crowds, military commands, brass bands, and the stamp and jingle of the march past of the Foot and Horse Guards. It must willingly go out on its own from the Palace into the Mall, facing without hesitation the almost tangible emotional barrier of the cheering that greets the Queen. Once positioned at the saluting base on Horseguards Parade it must stand quietly until it is time for the Queen to ride back to the Palace at the head of the Queen's Guard. It has to be a horse that is neither too spirited for the stresses of the occasion, nor so unalert to its surroundings that it could easily be startled.

For a long while the Mounted Branch of the Metropolitan Police had the honour of supplying the Queen's charger for this ceremonial parade, and two of the horses, first Winstone and then Imperial, became well-known public 'figures'. Then some years ago the Royal Canadian Mounted Police presented the Queen with Burmese, a black mare from amongst those still bred and trained at Fort Walsh for the Mounties' celebrated musical ride, and she has since been ridden at the Trooping. In addition to being exemplary on parade, like all police horses Burmese is an exceptionally well-schooled and enjoyable ride, and she spends much of the year at Windsor taking her turn with Cossack and Bellboy. Now that the Royal Canadian Mounted Police have presented the Queen with another horse, a big black gelding called Centennial, handed over at Windsor in May 1977, Burmese may well relinquish her ceremonial duty and remain permanently at Windsor as a pleasure horse.

In addition to the riding horses at Windsor there are always a few young polo ponies and carriage horses being trained and yet to prove themselves. At Balmoral the Queen still breeds and keeps some Highland ponies, the type so beloved by Queen Victoria, and also Fells, the 'aliens' first introduced in Scotland by King George VI. They were so-called because, not being indigenous, they were originally much resented imports. Nowadays there are Haflingers as well, as the Queen was given a pair of mares of this attractive flaxen-maned-and-tailed sturdy mountain pony breed when on a state visit to Austria in 1969.

The royal horse breeding at Sandringham was all begun at the Queen's instigation. From time to time one or other of the state carriage horses in the royal mews at Buckingham Palace has been home-bred, and for years the Queen tried, mostly with small success, to breed the type of polo pony Prince Philip liked to play. The Queen is one of the few acknowledged world authorities on the intricate subject of thoroughbred blood lines, and each season she works out the mating programmes for her own brood mares. Often she then has the satisfaction and added interest of following the racing fortunes of some animal that is the result of her own calculations. The Queen's delightful filly Highclere, by Queen's Hussar, the sire of Brigadier Gerard, won the 1,000 Guineas and the French Oaks, and holds the monetary record won in one year by a filly trained in England. Highclere's first foal, a colt, is by the inimitable little Mill Reef, one of the great mile-and-a-half horses of all time, and should therefore have a bright future ahead of him.

The famous royal stallion Aureole, impeccably bred, and sired by the great Hyperion, was inherited by the Queen from her father, King George VI. In his early racing days the fiery chestnut's antics at the starting post were a byword, but his speed and ability combined with the jockey Eph Smith's horsemanship and exceptionally light hands to make this a notable partnership. In all Aureole won seven races, with a wonderful season as a four-year-old, which included winning the Coronation Cup at Epsom and the valuable King George VI and Queen Elizabeth Stakes, but his greatest triumphs were at stud. Aureole stood at the Queen's Wolferton Stud, near Sandringham, for many years. He was leading sire in both 1960 and 1961, and by 1973 had fathered the winners of five hundred races all over the world, to the value of a million pounds.

The Queen's enthusiasm for racing began when, as Princess Elizabeth, she became joint owner with her mother, Queen Elizabeth, of a steeplechaser called Monaveen. This was not long before the King died, and after his death the new Queen's racing interests switched to the flat, while the Queen Mother gradually became a knowledgeable and lasting devotee of 'chasing.

The first horse ever to carry the Queen Mother's now famous racing colours was Manicou. The horse, French-bred, belonged originally to Lord Mildmay and was passed on after his owner's death. A brilliant steeplechaser, Manicou's last and greatest win was the King George VI Chase at Kempton Park where, still only a five-year-old, he beat the subsequent Gold Cup winner, Silver Fame. Manicou sired many famous horses, including the Queen Mother's well known The Rip, that she bought from a publican in the north. Through the years there have been other well known names, such as Laffy and Makaldar, to bring success and enjoyment to their royal owner, but nowadays only about five horses are kept in training, with a few young ones coming along at Hampton Court.

Because 'chasers only start to race when they are considerably more mature than those that compete on the flat, there are usually more 'characters' amongst a 'chasing string and the Queen Mother's is no exception. Like the Queen she is extremely knowledgeable about all facets of her sport, and of horses in general. She takes the greatest interest in her 'chasers as 'personalities', and goes to see them in the stable as often as she can. Game Spirit, bought on the recommendation of a handicapper who had been studying his form, won twenty-one races for his owner, more than any of her others, and even beat the mighty Bula at Newbury in 1977. But this wasn't the only reason why the Queen Mother was fond of him. She loved the horse for his great heart that made him always try his best, and because he was a charming character to meet, known in the stables as a 'real Christian'. The giant 17·2 hands-high Isle of Man, a great tearaway and confirmed front runner, is another favourite, partly because he is the last of the Manicou line. And these two share their owner's special affections with Colman, a robust little chestnut that is no great 'chaser, but is another sired by Colonist II that has a most attractive and friendly personality.

Although Princess Margaret enjoys racing she is not as great an enthusiast as her mother and the Queen, but as a child she shared her sister's love of ponies. When the Princesses remained in Scotland at the beginning of the war, there was only a small staff and so they had the fun and enjoyment of looking after their own ponies with minimum help. They taught them several tricks – standing up with front hooves on a garden seat was one – not usually included in a pony's training. The Queen claims that her own, a bronze-coloured, gay animal called Jock, taught her more than any other horse, and the same might be said of her sister's Norwegian pony, Hans.

Prince Charles, before the start of Ascot 1976.

Princess Margaret and her children always ride when they are at Balmoral during the summer holiday in Scotland, and the Princess frequently uses one of the horses in the mews at Windsor. For a long time her favourite was Agreement, a well-known racehorse belonging to the Queen who came to Windsor about 1964 when his legs would not stand up to further racing. Something of a rogue in his youth (he had to be gelded after he had savaged another horse when out on exercise), Agreement included the Doncaster Cup amongst his winnings, but when first at Windsor he was not everyone's idea of a good hack. He appeared to be very lazy and it was hard work to make him keep up with the other horses on exercise, although as well to do so. If allowed to lag too far behind, Agreement was not above putting in a hefty buck before setting off to demonstrate his race-winning speed – only to brake suddenly, and occasionally disastrously, directly he drew alongside his leading stablemate. However, by the time Princess Margaret was able to form a good partnership with the unpredictable chestnut, some intensive schooling had cured him of most of his foibles – although he was still inclined to put his rider's teeth on edge by continuously grinding his own.

Prince Edward, Lady Sarah Armstrong-Jones and Viscount Linley in Windsor Great Park.

Prince Philip, like his daughter a 'doer' rather than a 'looker on', is no great racing fan. Until his fiftieth birthday, when recurring wrist trouble confirmed him in his intention to give up polo at that age, the game provided him with all the excitement and violent exercise he liked and needed. When the two elder children were quite young there were occasional family riding parties in the park, and Prince Philip usually rode Mele-Kush, a kindly dispositioned stallion of the speedy Akhal-teke desert breed given him by Mr Khrushchev. When polo and practice took up all the time the Prince could spare for riding, and Mele-Kush proved to be no use at stud, the horse was taken on by a lady rider, who competed with him enjoyably and with some success in show-jumping and other competitions at riding club level.

Prince Philip kept his polo pony string in the yard that bears his name just inside the main gateway at the Windsor mews. The majority of his ponies were Argentine bred, a few of the stamp of his excellent Noche Dia, a heavyweight that combined quite good speed with maximum co-operation. There were usually two or three home-breds from Sandringham out-of ex-polo pony mares, but sad to say Prince Philip seldom formed a successful partnership with them. At one point he did have hopes of Bullseye, a curious, lop-eared pony with a zany expression, but they came to nothing. Lightning was another, possessing all the speed and ability of a first-class pony, but liable to work herself into such a frenzy during a game that her exasperated owner nick-named her 'The Idiot Woman!'

The most treasured and best known of all was what is now something of a rarity, a high-class English thoroughbred pony, in this case a granddaughter of Hyperion and bred by Lord Rosebery. Betaway was very sensitive by nature – Prince Philip used to say that if he was rude to this mare she would promptly retaliate by standing on her hind legs – and like most blood animals her hot temperament could make her less handy than an Argentine pony. But on the straight there was nothing to touch her; open the throttle and away she went. In fact Betaways' speed was so phenomenal that she became something of a legend on the polo-ground, and with press and public alike.

For some time before actually giving up polo, Prince Philip had been looking around for another sport to take its place. His interest centred on driving, something he reckoned he could do for many years to come, and particularly in the competitive form that had been popular on the continent for many years. And it is largely owing to his efforts and those of the Crown Equerry that there has been such a resurgence of interest in this country in the art of driving. Competitive driving follows rules standardised by a committee of the Federation Equestre Internationale in 1969 (Prince Philip is its President), and is an up-and-coming and popular sport.

Prince Philip now devotes to his new sport the time he used to spend practicing and playing polo, but it has to be fitted in with the immense number of public commitments he undertakes annually. And when it is compared with the dedicated daily hours of practice put in by other top competitors, it says much for Prince Philip's prowess and enthusiasm that he is able to drive, and win, in the best company.

He practices whenever he can at weekends at Windsor, and during the royal family's Christmas holiday at Sandringham tries to get out with his team three or four times in the week for quite long periods. On a Sunday his own and his horses' problems are increased by posses of amateur photographers standing in their path to get a better picture!

The Princes' team of four are chosen from the six horses always kept in work, with another taken along as reserve when travelling to compete. In the 1973–74 season the team consisted of one pure-bred Cleveland Bay and four part-breds, but these have gradually been replaced by better bred British horses and some from Germany. As with most active sports there is a spice of danger about competitive driving, but Prince Philip has no more spills than other competitors and they are usually less dramatic than the press would have us believe. Both he and his horses have learned to cope with hazards as part of the day's work, and even water obstacles, which look so spectacular when a four-in-hand is splashing through, unless they are encountered somewhere unexpected, such as in a dark wood, are taken in their stride.

These horses do receive one form of training not accorded to those of other competitors. To acclimatise them to crowds and military music they are often driven along behind the band going up for Changing of the Guard at Windsor Castle, while all onlookers are encouraged to cheer. This is because these horses are not kept specifically for Prince Philip to drive. They are always used on ceremonial occasions, just like any other animals kept in the royal mews at Buckingham Palace. And it says much for their training that they are as steady and reliable drawing a state coach down the Mall for some great public occasion, as they are taking part in the tests of presentation and dressage, marathon and obstacle driving, demanded under the three tables of an F.E.I. driving competition.

Doublet was somewhat aloof, if gentlemanly, in the stable. He gave of his best in all three phases of an event, with a special flair for dressage, unlike Goodwill who, although much improved in the dressage arena, can still give the impression of a volcano about to blow his top. Goodwill is in fact a much stronger, more robust horse, of a totally different stamp, who can pull with the best across country. And although, like him, Doublet was agile, honest and brave, he did not possess the seemingly endless scope, particularly over spreads, of the ex-show jumper with which Princess Anne came fourth at Badminton in 1974, twelfth in the World Championships, second in the 1975 European Championships, and completed all phases of the 1976 Olympic three-day event.

The Duke of Edinburgh driving in the coaching marathon in Windsor Great Park 1975.

Between them the Princess and Captain Phillips have the fun and interest of schooling, competing with and enjoying a variety of different horses. One of the most controversial is Columbus, the giant grey, bred by the Queen, with which Anne won an intermediate class of a one-day event in 1972. Always a tough guy – take a look at Columbus in his box and he jumps up and down with flattened ears and bared teeth – when he grew too powerful for a girl rider, Mark took him on, although with small success in 1973. By the next year Mark was convinced this was an Olympic horse and they won Badminton in 1974. But when leading individually in the World Championships at Burghley the horse had to be withdrawn with a hock injury. This recurred in 1976 to preclude any thought of Montreal, but by the next spring Columbus was again in work, being ridden by Mark, to a future that might include show jumping if not eventing.

Mark considers no horse can equal a thoroughbred. His own special joy is the seventeen hands-high, well-bred Persian Holiday (Percy in the family), with which he was placed in all thirteen events they contested together during 1973–74, and which he took to the Olympics as one of the reserve horses. Mark could never understand why his wife did not enjoy her blood horse Arthur of Troy – sold in 1977 – but Anne always felt that though Arthur had a lot of ability he and she were just not compatible! This is certainly not so with the less aristocratic Flame Gun, a cocky little chestnut who is not unlike Goodwill to ride. Flame missed Badminton 1976 through lameness and has yet to prove himself over the 'big stuff', Braham could have been the venue in 1977 but for the royal baby.

Like all top notch event riders these two have young horses coming along. Mark's Cassette, a very sensitive chestnut gelding, won their first novice one-day event in 1976, and was open standard by the following spring. His bay Drumwill is by the same sire as the Olympic horse Playamar, and had much the same phlegmatic outlook, but is now 'jollying up'.

When they were quite young Prince Charles and Princess Anne both had ponies. Later they shared an admirable Welsh pony called Bandit, and he taught them quite a lot about competing in Pony Club gymkhanas. When Bandit was outgrown, Charles, never as interested as Anne, or as talented – and not always appreciative of the plentiful advice proffered by a younger sister – gave up riding until he was about fifteen. Eventually he was lured back into the saddle by the attractions of polo, his first efforts encouraged by the sense and wisdom of two elderly polo ponies, San Quinina, belonging to his father, and Sombra, a present from Lord Cowdray.

Despite time being limited by royal duties and service in the Navy, Prince Charles has developed into a very useful player. He now keeps three ponies, two home-bred – which must please the Queen – and an Argentine. Apart from playing and practicing whenever possible, the Prince of Wales enjoys an occasional day with hounds and is beginning to show some interest in driving.

After Bandit, Princess Anne acquired High Jinks a 14.2 hands-high Irish bred, sensible 'family' type of pony, that arrived at Windsor as a four-year-old. They formed an excellent partnership, slowly finding their way together. Neither knew much about competing, but rider and pony shared a love of galloping and jumping small fences across country – with few troubles except for the ditches to which Jinks at first took exception. Before very long they were doing quite well in Pony Club hunter trials.

Purple Star, Anne's first horse, was small and lively, inexperienced but with much promise, and, under Alison Oliver's wise and expert training, exactly right for partnering the Princess in the early stages. A great 'character', Purple was always ready, given the chance, to buck in a dressage arena, or, as in the 1971 Windsor Horse Trials, show his displeasure at being 'pushed' extra hard at water – never a favourite hazard – by an exaggerated leap that took his rider for a swim. As Anne became ruefully aware, if he thought fit Purple could stop at a show fence with unseating speed, but although too small for a three-day eventer he had graduated to open one-day events by 1970. When he began stopping at cross-country fences, the Princess decided to retire the little horse to hunting, a sport he thoroughly enjoys.

The two horses, one sadly dead, with which Princess Anne made her way into the world's top ranking event riders, were very dissimilar. Doublet, tragically to break a leg at exercise in 1974, was in at the beginning; he was a rather difficult young horse bred by the Queen as a polo pony, who grew too big and was sent to Alison Oliver as a possible event horse for the Princess. Both demanding and rewarding, he was considered by Alison to be just right for her pupil at that stage. At first doubtful, Anne accepted the challenge, and she and Doublet soon formed a relationship of mutual trust and understanding that took them to the top in a remarkably short while. They came fifth at Badminton in 1971, their first three-day event, and went on to win the individual title in the European Championships that same autumn.

Anne decided they would have to part with her beloved Mardi Gras, by the Queen Mother's Manicou, which she fell off more times than any other horse. But much as she enjoyed him, they just had too many horses. She is bringing on the Irish Inchiguin who was bought in the autumn of 1976, and made his debut in the following spring, and Golden Reel, very naughty and with a penchant for bucking, that she and Mark bought as a three-year-old and broke in themselves.

Goodwill, after a well deserved rest, was starting work again by January 1977, but he will be too old for the 1980 Olympics. If Princess Anne can find another horse of his ability, her own ambitions, as well as those of her husband, may well be fulfilled – to be chosen once more for the British Olympic team.

Having cleared this
Cheltenham fence,
Biddlecombe's 150 pounds
thump back into
Trelawney's saddle.

17 TERRY BIDDLECOMBE
The style is the man

Rob Hughes

When the 18th century Comte de Buffon wrote those words he could hardly have foreseen English National Hunt jockey Terry Biddlecombe coming down the home straight. Yet the Frenchman's quote is apt because Biddlecombe was for seventeen seasons a flamboyant D'Artagnan of the English track. And the manner of Biddlecombe's riding was indeed the true man: unorthodox, compulsively reckless and gutsy, honest to the core.

His riding style, the way he perched on a horse, had off-beat pedigree too: it was the only point of similarity between ebullient Biddlecombe and the frowning, taciturn champion flat jockey Lester Piggott. Both had their legs tucked beneath them in short leathers, knees hugging the horse's mane, backsides almost comically pitched towards the heavens. 'Helped balance a horse,' says Biddlecombe, denying it was too precarious a style to stay aboard when horses crashed down at forty miles an hour. His 'hands and heels' riding had evolved in apple-in-the-bucket pony club events after he began jumping fences on his father's Cotswolds farm at five.

Biddlecombe's career (1957–58 to 1973–74) pitted him against some of the great National Hunt jockeys, and many whose bravery was a fine madness. Terry was champion three times; but for injury he would have doubled that. His 912 winners were ridden with a talent which cannot be taught, in a fashion few would copy, with a nerve fewer still could surpass. Nobody met fences with greater commitment, or rode horses harder for the finish; nobody enjoyed race riding more, a paradox considering the price he had to pay in numerous bloody instalments. Astonishingly Biddlecombe squeezed lively fun from the kind of danger that curdles most men's stomachs; the luminous smile survived even when it sometimes seemed his natural position was dangling, rodeo fashion, upside down beneath a falling horse's neck. But determination could also clamp his lips into a tight grim line as he balanced a horse, ushering it clinically towards a fence and, with a huge cry of 'Ga'arn,' kicking it into a jump.

'Everything was a challenge,' he reflects. 'That's what I loved in a race. The art was to jump fences well, get a length advantage here and there. If you didn't jump them, too bloody bad – you ended up in hospital or something. But if you didn't try to jump better than the rest, you never won a thing.'

He didn't jump them all. We first met, in 1970, in a hospital after I'd rung ward C.3 of Ashford Hospital, Middlesex about a television interview. Terry's richly-accented Gloucestershire voice was deceptively cheery: 'Feeling marvellous, great. Can't wait to get back. Cracked a couple of ribs or something. Be here a day or so, I reckon.' The eye gave the truth: Biddlecombe lying uneasily propped up by a small mountain of pillows; savage pain had made a chalk mask of those blond, fresh features which normally made him look startlingly like a Jack Nicklaus of the saddle. His eyes watered and deep grinding breaths cut from time to time into his conversation. When he tried once or twice to laugh his ribs punished him with that fierce stab that amateur National Hunt jockey Lord Oaksey once described as 'like a flick-knife in the chest'.

In the corridor outside waited Bridget Biddlecombe, Terry's wife of two years and already veteran of too many hospital visits. Her husband had the pain but Bridget was gripped by something perhaps worse – fear. From the day of their engagement he had promised to name the date of his retirement: it was always 'just two more years'. Meantime Bridget, a former show jumper, brought with her a spectre on each hospital visit: the memory of a meeting she'd had with a brain-damaged former jockey.

This time her husband was nearer death than he will ever admit. Immediately after the fall, King's Dream, his novice mount, had knelt his full half-ton weight into the small of Biddlecombe's back and then rolled on top of him. Ribs were crushed, and a kidney so severely bruised he passed blood with his urine for three weeks.

In the hospital ward, Terry narrated for the camera a spectacular fall he had shrugged off seven years previously. His blithe recital, in the best Dawn Patrol manner was, I suspect, catharsis for dark emotions he did not care to probe too closely.

'I fell at the water jump. Stratford, I think it was . . . the horse got up, and my foot caught in the stirrup and the horse started trotting. I couldn't grab him and, suddenly, after he'd gone a furlong, he was getting into top gear and I was still being dragged. Next thing I saw a fence coming up . . . but . . . 'bout ten or fifteen yards from the fence the saddle slipped and my foot came loose. Just in time.

'I was only a kid . . . rode in the next race. Mind you, I woke up once or twice that night thinking my leg was being pulled out of joint or something.

It was only nightmares, no harm done. It's not the spectacular falls that hurt'.

There's a saying that, in National Hunt, you're a jockey for five years; after that you just ride around. After five years, they look to see if your nerve has gone. Biddlecombe had proved again and again that his nerve may have matured but wasn't done. He went on proving it for another four years after those cruel 1970 injuries, surviving a chilling catalogue of 350 falls, thirty-eight broken bones, and some fifty times being scooped off racetracks and bundled, often unconscious, into ambulances, then sped to infirmaries.

Despite this list, Terry was no clumsier nor more brittle than other accomplished jump jockeys. He thought his average of being dumped heavily from horses about twenty-two times a season 'par for the course'. The most illustrious spent much time, mudstained and grimacing, stretched out in wailing ambulances. Fred 'Mr Grand National' Winter hit the deck forty-one times in the 1952–53 season; Stan 'The Bounce' Mellor suffered ten separate facial fractures in one fall at Aintree in 1963 and had 400 falls in twenty-one seasons; Jack 'Boneless Wonder' Dowdeswell, the outstanding jump jockey before and after World War II, stopped counting his broken bones after tallying fifty-two and spills over 500.

Quietly, without parading the fact, these small men are more stoical than Apaches; the Freudian school would perhaps sum it up as a virility factor. Yet even tough nuts blanched at one of Biddlecombe's exploits. In 1964, a few hours after a tumble had chipped two inches from a shoulder blade, a trainer, and then a doctor rang his home to find out how he was faring. 'Sorry,' answered his father, 'Terry's gone for a spot of shooting in the Malverns. He gets a bit bored sitting around'.

Suppressed pain, can, however, lead men like Biddlecombe to cross the invisible frontier that separates stoicism from foolhardiness. In 1971, as the two of us sprinted for a taxi in London, Terry suddenly went white around the gills. 'Got this bruising in my back,' he explained. Three days before, following a heavy fall, he had driven home, swallowed a couple of Dispirin, and returned the next day to ride a winner in one of three races – after riding out for three hours that morning. When his ailment, all-too-easily diagnosed as 'bruising', persisted, X-rays showed the frightening truth: two cracked vertebrae.

To have emerged from jump racing as something more than hamburger, Biddlecombe had to become a considerable master of the jockey's art of curling up into a tight ball, like a hedgehog, arms protecting head, in the split second between landing and being used as a doormat by the ensuing hooves. Significantly, not one of his thirty-eight fractures was around the head or neck, and only two were below the belt. He took the impact and punishment through the shoulders and arms: twenty-three of his fractures were in those regions.

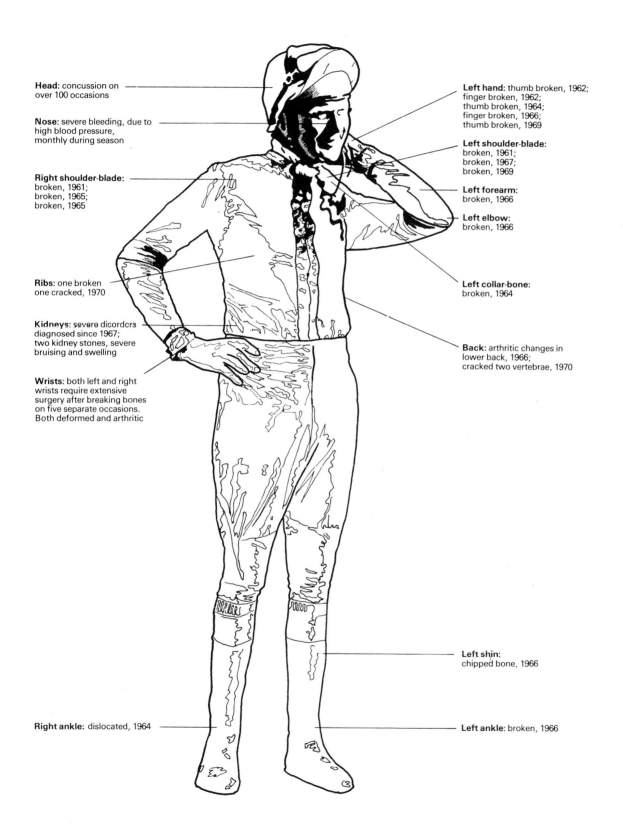

Head: concussion on over 100 occasions

Nose: severe bleeding, due to high blood pressure, monthly during season

Right shoulder-blade: broken, 1961; broken, 1965; broken, 1965

Ribs: one broken one cracked, 1970

Kidneys: severe disorders diagnosed since 1967; two kidney stones, severe bruising and swelling

Wrists: both left and right wrists require extensive surgery after breaking bones on five separate occasions. Both deformed and arthritic

Left hand: thumb broken, 1962; finger broken, 1962; thumb broken, 1964; finger broken, 1966; thumb broken, 1969

Left shoulder-blade: broken, 1961; broken, 1967; broken, 1969

Left forearm: broken, 1966

Left elbow: broken, 1966

Left collar-bone: broken, 1964

Back: arthritic changes in lower back, 1966; cracked two vertebrae, 1970

Left shin: chipped bone, 1966

Right ankle: dislocated, 1964

Left ankle: broken, 1966

Physical jeopardy, alas, did not end with fractured limbs, throbbing head-pains or bruised body organs. In February 1970, a week before the fall which put him into Ashford hospital, Biddlecombe was draped over a chair in Chepstow racetrack's first-aid room, his pale body a pincushion absorbing syringe needles to numb pain and restore strength and balance.

Terry, then twenty-nine, had not fallen from his mount. In his fourteenth season he was paying the penalty for having fecklessly abused his metabolism for half his lifetime. Earlier a frozen crowd had cheered him around two laps of tough, undulating track, over three and a half miles and twenty-two demanding fences and tenacious finish to win the Welsh Grand National on French Excuse. In the winners' enclosure he had to be lifted from the saddle, blood pouring from his nose.

'Nothing serious' recalled Biddlecombe, who could give Norman Vincent Peale lessons in positive thinking, 'I'd wasted hard to ten stone nine (149 pounds) and got a little exhausted. Actually, I'd put a bit too much into the race and had cramp something terrible in my stomach. I couldn't see, felt a bit giddy. It'd happened before, two maybe three times – it's the long chases over three and a half miles. But a couple of Guinnesses afterwards and you're flying again, 'specially when you won'. All this delivered with beaming smile and throwaway nonchalance that takes years to perfect.

But Biddlecombe could be jarred. In May 1970 a young jockey named Fred Dixon, married and with a three-year-old son, broke his neck at Chepstow, the fourth rider to die on the track since Terry began racing. His first reaction was to contribute to a fund for Dixon's widow; his second to ride at the very next meeting, trying for maybe a dozen races to control fears slicing into his mind. 'I never thought about a really crippling injury. If you're going to get one, you're going to get it. Start worrying, and it's time to give up. Otherwise you make mistakes.'

As a Gulliver among Lilliputians, Biddlecombe was compelled to take risks. He discarded even the flimsiest protective equipment. For a fanatic, trimming off a few ounces this way seemed more profitable than protecting bones. Terry rationalized: 'I didn't ride with the intention of falling off. Didn't feel right all passed up around the back and shoulders – like some bloody American footballer.'

His size. Here was *the* problem. More than any other leading jockey, Biddlecombe was physically ill-equipped for the job. His sturdy frame, stretching up to 5 feet 10¾ inches, could carry a natural 12½ stones (175 pounds). Rivals, such as Stan Mellor, were natural bantamweights of little more than eight stones (112 pounds). Terry could do nothing about the frame but courted grievous and possibly permanent harm to keep 28 pounds under a healthy weight.

Most jockeys diet to beat the scales; Biddlecombe's challenge to his constitution pushed limits further than others dared or needed to: for the

This diagram illustrates the physical beating that Biddlecombe has taken in a career of top class racing.

ten-month racing season his breakfast was one cup of tea, no sugar; he ate nothing else until evening, when he sat down at inconsistent hours, to steak or fish or poultry with salad and a single glass of wine.

The dedicated voice. 'I brainwashed myself against food. But a few times I let go – fat, juicy steaks and champagne. Great. Next morning I bloody well paid, dropping six or seven pounds at the Turkish baths in Gloucester'.

Three saunas a week gave him the cleanest pores in racing, and helped cut his weight to the bone at ten stone eight pounds (148 pounds). Still it did not pare him enough: one pound can slow a horse a length over two miles, and trainer Fred Rimell assessed: 'I could have given Terry easily another hundred rides a season if he could have gotten below ten stones (140 pounds)'.

Terry's attitude was dangerously cavalier: I used to take a pill each morning to take away my appetite. One pill could shed anything from four to seven pounds. Pee pills they were – reckon I got to know every layby toilet in Britain. I stopped taking 'em when me kidneys hurt something terrible.'

Biddlecombe later suffered two kidney stones, each about half the size of a pea. Here were echoes of Bobby Beasley, pilot of the 1960 champion hurdle and 1961 Grand National winners, who had to retire prematurely in 1968 with inflated glands, sapped strength and numbed limbs. These were, Beasley thought, legacies of gulping dehydrating drugs which act on the kidneys to increase fluid loss.

Clear-eyed in retrospect, Biddlecombe sees the alarming hazards of riding ten months a year 21 pounds below his natural weight. In retirement, he can understand that persistent 'rests' that injuries forced on him gave his tortured system badly-needed respite. It is interesting to note that his first kidney stone appeared around 1965 and 1966, seasons when relative freedom from injury allowed him to become the only National Hunt jockey to ride 100 winners back-to-back. Was it also coincidence that a further eighteen months without disabling injury (1967–68) ended with a 'chill on the kidneys'. Or was it that savage, constant, wasting dehydrating pills and artificial sweat loss debilitated his plumbing? A wiser Biddlecombe now shrugs off the suggestion with less abandon than he used to.

Money could no more compensate the soul for such physical disarray than it could cushion the body against falls. 'Nobody rode steeples for money', Biddlecombe admits, 'Being a top jockey, I could reckon on maybe £6,000 (then $15,000) in a good year. That didn't leave a fortune after paying out for driving 50,000 miles a year, saddles, boots, breeches, valet fees, tax and insurance.' The 1970 fall cost him 200 rides (at £13.50 a mount, a loss of £2,700 (then $6,750); the $7\frac{1}{2}$ per cent cut of winner's fees; and his championship.

Yet even these frustrations did not sag Terry's spirit. 'I loved racing. Wouldn't have traded jumping, even for the Derby. Even though I'd have enjoyed the money on the flat. I'd have been a – bloody hell – perhaps even a millionaire.' By contrast, the flat racing champion who most shared Biddlecombe's agonies over fasting, Lester Piggott, paid more tax in a single year than Terry saved in his career. It is a neat and ironic co-incidence that this pair, to whom 'food' was the true four-letter word, were the strongest-finishing riders of their time. Biddlecombe also tantalised punters and agitated owners by leaving his challenge to the last, a habit he telegraphed at seventeen on his first winner, beating champion Fred Winter by a short head at Wincanton in 1958.

Biddlecombe was raised within a sharp gallop of the Cheltenham course, venue for one of National Hunt's two great races. The Cheltenham Gold Cup, highlight of the West country festival each March, is the supreme test at level weights to determine the best stayer in the land over three and a quarter miles. The other classic is, of course, the Grand National held at Aintree, Liverpool each April, attracting television millions who rarely heed horseracing of any type. Overcrowded, handicapped fields of forty or more runners frequently produce mêlees of cartwheeling horseflesh and airborne riders at the thirty massive fences scattered over four and a half miles.

Terry's appraisal of the two races may have stemmed from pain as well as home-town prejudice. 'For me the Cheltenham Gold Cup is the greatest steeplechase in the world; the National is a lottery. The Gold Cup's a real test, a truer race between you and twenty others on the best horses in racing, with no luck involved. Greatest thrill of my life, winning at Cheltenham. It was never an ambition of mine to win the National – you need luck to finish, never mind bloody win'.

Cheltenham's searching four-furlong uphill finish suited Biddlecombe's strength. He won the Gold Cup on Woodland Venture in 1967 (with an injected bruised thigh), was unluckily beaten one and a half lengths on Domacorn in 1969 (after losing his whip) and finished unplaced only once in seven Gold Cups.

His snarled remark on the National ('never been good to me') was an understatement. He never won it; in fact he finished in only three of eight attempts; (Mellor had no victory in fifteen attempts). Aintree was Terry's bloody battleground. In 1961 his first Grand National experience was a broken left wrist, shoulder and hand; his horse Tokoroa had to be destroyed. In 1964 he suffered concussion, internal injury and splintered two fingers, a collar-bone and arm. He finished fourth in 1967, after being halted behind the bittest pile-up in National history at the twenty-third jump.

In 1970–71–72 his vexing experiences all involved a horse whose name, Gay Trip, was a rancid irony. First he watched on hospital television as Pat Taafe substituted and *won* the National; in 1971 he and Gay Trip came a cropper at the first; then he finished his final Aintree classic in second place – more annoyed than before. 'My fellow gave the winner twenty-two pounds. The T.V. cameras missed it, but some bugger fell, stopped us dead in our tracks, and left us ten to fifteen lengths to make up. It was too much to ask the little horse'.

All aspects, except the result, were right when Biddlecombe rode his last race on March 14, 1974. It was at Cheltenham, in the Gold Cup aboard the Queen Mother's perfectly-named horse, Game Spirit. But life is no Frank Capra film; Terry's driving effort could achieve only third place for his emotion-choked supporters. Then the summing-up:

'Racing has been good to me. I've come out without brain damage or anything like that. I've had marvellous times. Only time I felt miserable was after wasting hard on a cold day, with sleet driving hard into my face and an east wind cutting me in half at the start before a three-and-a-half mile race. But once I got going, the thrill took over'.

Biddlecombe had carved an astonishing career, only put into perspective when you remember his ever-present weight handicap. Stan Mellor (the only National Hunt rider to win 1,000 races) and Fred Winter (923) beat Terry's 912 winners; Josh Gifford's record 122 winners in a season was better than Terry's 117 (although he remains the only rider with successive centuries); Winter and Gifford each won four National Hunt titles to Biddlecombe's three (Terry was three times squeezed out by a couple of winners to new champions who'd piled up winners as he lay in hospital).

In the wake of retirement at thirty-three he had a new life to build for a family that now included Laurie, aged one, and a baby sister Elizabeth. Farming? Well . . . horses really had to be the centre of things.

High in the saddle in 1967, Terry Biddlecombe (*right*) coaxes Woodland Venture over the last fence past Stalbridge Colonist to go on and win his favourite race, the Cheltenham Gold Cup.

Grand ideas – a training yard for Mr – a show-jump school for Mrs – were not to be. 'I hadn't started to mend my ways soon enough; preferred a good time and saved next to nothing. Even if I had, inflation would have done for us. They were asking £60,000 to £100,000 ($120,000 to $200,000) for thirty boxes and a bit of paddock land.'

So they compromised, used the bit of land around their splendid detached Gloucester home, and a nearby 24-acre plot, containing sixteen horseboxes and a small indoor training arena (into which their entire savings were invested) to set up as equestrian odd-job specialists . . . 'doing anything and everything with horses – breaking 'em in, schooling, making sound, patching up – anything trainers hadn't time to do'.

After back-breaking labour, it was in full swing within a year. 'We've everything in the yard, from a broken-down old mare to an English Derby prospect. One came written-off, had an operation and with good care returned to win three races'.

Overlooking the fence between his back door and paddock, one animal responded knowingly to Biddlecombe's voice. 'Coral Diver,' he said, 'best horse I sat on; won £21,000 with me up. Bryan Jenks (owner) said he was mine when he finished racing but I got a call saying he's split a tendon, would be shot. We brought him here, treated him lightly with acid fire (a technique to seal the crack) and he's so bloody well now we put him with the old mare to quieten him down. Might hunt him later'.

Biddlecombe's left leg looked stiff when he swung himself into the saddle. Arthritis? 'Nah. I've got some of that, but the trouble is the young ill-tempered buggers I get to sort out. In sixteen years' schooling I'd been bucked maybe ten times . . . but this young so-and-so threw me, cracked three ribs, bruised my hip and chipped the inside of a knee-cap. I got back on, gave him the biggest hiding I've given a horse. Good as gold he is now'.

His forty-second fracture (a finger while keeping wicket for the National Hunt cricketers' XI) roused talk of retiring from cricket, talk perhaps as idle as his 15-year muttering about having a surgeon break and re-set horrendously warped wrists, bent through riding before breakages mended.

He has blinkered his thoughts from that, just as he has switched off bad memories: of having horses die under him; of eight jockey friends who died (four on the track, four in car crashes on the endlessly fatiguing journeys, sometimes feeling the day's ill-effects); of colleagues maimed by their profession; of good men he rode alongside and watched end up total destitute and broken.

These dark areas smear somewhat his surging love for National Hunt. But ask what he would like to be remembered for and his answer is stunningly, sweetly simple: 'A fun jockey. That was the aim.'

From Biddlecombe those words have the 'ping' of struck crystal. But let Lester Piggott try to use them some day as an exit line.

18 WHAT MAKES SCOBIE RUN

Brough Scott

Scobie Breasley was a very special jockey. In racing's history he was only the second man to have carved long and brilliantly successful riding careers in two different countries. Different hemispheres in fact. In his first career, which lasted just over twenty years, he proved himself a superlative jockey in his native Australia. Then moving towards the dangerous age of forty he blocked out the sneers of the pessimists and came to England for what turned out to be a second and even more potent ration of glory – eighteen seasons, two Derby wins, four jockey's championships and always that unmistakable style, with its hunched precise finesse that became his signature across the racing world.

The only other two-hemispheres champion was the extraordinary Rae 'Togo' Johnstone who, a generation before Breasley, knew laurels and champagne both in Australia and France. Yet even Johnstone's accomplishments did not match Breasley's overall success in racing because Scobie went on to become a far more significant trainer. But training, his third phase, surprisingly brought some unexpected and unearned agonies to a man who could, if he'd chosen, have tugged on his houndstooth cap and walked away from it all without a backward glance.

What made Scobie run? And what was it – hope, cussedness, stoicism, true grit – that kept this veteran battling on as a racehorse trainer when fate and other agencies had him leapfrogging in and out of three racing worlds in fifteen months during the late 1970s.

In terms of money and honours, Scobie Breasley didn't have to put up with this buffeting and uncertainty. He already had behind him half a century of lucrative success as a champion jockey, one of the best ever in Australia and Britain; altogether he rode more than 3,000 winners. He could have spent his autumn years lounging bare chested on the patio of his Barbados retreat, sipping the odd Gibson and scanning an airmail copy of *Sporting Life*. Yet,

Ballymoss ridden by Scobie Breasley is led in after winning the King George and Queen Elizabeth stakes at Ascot in 1958.

153

in his seventh decade, Breasley wittingly, and in quick succession, hurled himself into two new briar patches with very long thorns – the savagely competitive trainer's life in France and then the United States.

The 1976 season turned out to be his only one training out of Chantilly, Europe's richest training centre in the old château town just twenty miles up the N.16 motorway from Paris. It was a more triumphant season than the turf oracles of England and France, and perhaps Scobie himself, had anticipated. But it ended swiftly and sourly. An official accusation and disqualification of a horse after an important victory jolted him and made dispassionate, but worried, observers blow their noses on the Tricolour. These setbacks also tripped off the volatile temper of his boss, Ravi Tikkoo, who yanked his horses out of Chantilly and immediately airfreighted them across the Atlantic.

Breasley and his thirty-six horses touched down in New York just before the start of the bitterest winter in recorded history; the state would be feet deep in snow and ice. So the plucky Australian began the third phase of his training career with his horses and himself marooned inside the snowbound training complex at Belmont. It was enough to bring palpitations to the stoutest heart. But, luckily, Scobie had a good one pumping away inside his compact chest.

Clearly the ingredients fuelling Breasley to accept, then survive, all this unsettling migration combined into a high-octane fuel. Among the most potent were optimism, oft-revealed courage, the driving instincts of a natural competitor, and – the best quality of all – sheer class. No other jockey anywhere has shown his unmistakable class as naturally and easily as Breasley does every time he sits astride a racehorse. That lean and craggy Roman emperor's face (as sparsely topped as Caesar's), always kept a master's repose. Long after he hung up his silks those deft movements around the reins remained as firm but as gentle as his leathery handshake. The little figure hinged forward as balanced and controlled as a gold medal skier negotiating an icy piste. In the saddle, Scobie has always presented an aristocratic mien more akin to a Boston Brahmin or son of Arundel than to a man born (in 1914) the sixth of seven children in a sheep drover's family at Wagga Wagga, New South Wales. It was the surface aspect and the living proof of a God-given talent that graduated from wild pony busting, through a reign as monarch of Melbourne's Caulfield, and then champion and dual Epsom Derby winner in England.

As a boy and young man in the Australian bush he had dreamed of England as the ultimate riding arena, the setting for what was then literally the sport of kings. Breasley might well have ended his active racing days in England as a solidly successful trainer had he not teamed up, in the mid 1970s, with Ravi Tikkoo. The big, trim and immaculately barbered Tikkoo had, in the twenty years since he arrived in Britain from Kashmir, built one of the world's biggest oil tanker empires (and achieved much notoriety in 1977 when he sacked the Filipino crew of his tanker Globtik Venus at Le Havre and hired a batch of out-of-work British trawlermen to seize control of the ship). Early in 1974, before he became Breasley's chief patron, Tikkoo had already moved his racing string across the channel from England in protest against the 8½ per cent Value Added Tax operating on all bloodstock sales in Britain, but not in France and Ireland. The following winter Tikkoo brought the horses back but, eight months later he muttered: 'This (British) government really makes it impossible for someone like me to operate. I am afraid it looks as if we are going to have to move everything to France.' And he did.

'Everything' meant the fifty-eight horses formerly spread among three other trainers in England, France and Ireland. It meant taking over the pine-built establishment of Baron de Waldner on the Chemin-des-Aigles between Mathet and Rothschild, and the complementary stud twenty kilometres away. Above all, it meant getting Scobie to go with him.

At Breasley's elbow in the Tikkoo camp mooched his shrewd compatriot Bill Williamson, whose lack of obvious animation had long before brought him the nickname 'Weary Willie'. Lacklustre or not, Bill had stamped his world class as a rider throughout Europe, winning France's Arc de Triomphe in 1968 and 1969. After retiring in 1973 he imported his tact and knowledge into Tikkoo's racing set-up. While these two leathery old 'diggers' were a walking brains trust on racing, Breasley's trans-channel hop was a massive and puzzling gamble. Already he lived in near Regency grandeur at Epsom amid racing folk he had known for decades, all speaking a common tongue: English turf patois. His chocolate 'SB52' Rolls Royce whisked him wherever he wanted to go or elegantly encased his cheerful wife Mae and their two grandchildren on trips to London. Why should a near-pensioner uproot himself from all this to take on the world's finest Thoroughbreds surrounded by those frostily uncooperative French?

The simple reason was that, for any European trainer who loved a challenge, France in the mid-1970s had become the rainbow's end, the sport's promised land. Annual prize money had risen above £15 million, averaging almost £4,000 a race plus 30 per cent to owners of French breeds and 25 per cent premium to winning French breeders. By comparison, down-at-heel Britain had just £5 million in prize money and less than £2,000 a race. The bloom on French racing came from an enlightened betting taxation system yielding more than £80 million to racing and almost £154 million to the State from £908.5 million turnover. From Britain's Heath Robinson system dribbled £9 million for racing and £97 million to the Exchequer on £1,285.5 million turnover.

Individual comparisons were even more ludicrous. In 1975 England's exceptional Derby winner Grundy amassed £188,375, almost as good as the

£198,578 French Derby winner Val de l'Orne gathered to top their list. But Bolkonski, runner-up to Grundy with £64,000 in England, would not have made the first dozen in France. Worse still, Peter Walwyn's record-breaking English training aggregate of £382,527 would have put him only seventh behind Alex Head's £810,594 atop the French table. That year trainer Breasley finished eighth on the English charts, his best ever placing, with £68,788 from forty-five races won. Creditable but pitiful when placed alongside the £303,562 his French counterpart, Jean Michel de Choubersky, gained from just twenty-two successes.

Despite Breasley's achievements in England initial scepticism about the wisdom of his move hung heavier in the Chantilly air than winter mist. Seventy-eight-year-old Jack Honeywood, a head lad there for many years, cocked his parrot-like face in the Sylvia bar and mused over his Ricard: 'Everyone talks as if it will be easy for Scobie. But I am not so sure. There is a lot of competition here now . . . really big strings like Wildenstein's, Head's and Boutin's, who want to farm even the little races; they are very difficult to beat. And these Frenchmen are difficult to mix with. Scobie doesn't speak the language; he won't even know the system of training or be able to speak to the lads'.

Honeywood had made many good points. From 1970 to 1975 the number of horses at Chantilly and neighbouring villages had leapt from 1,370 to 3,440 and the horseracing population up to 75 trainers and 1,500 assorted workers; turf and sand gallops had spread from 110 hectares to 200. Trainers had more facilities but a much more difficult task in learning their terrain and coping with nuisances like coming at full stride across a string of horses galloping the opposite way down the same paths. What had not been diluted or smothered were Chantilly's visible English connections: the cockney pernod accents of retired old timers who'd been imported as apprentices in the 1920s: the Head family guarding their English origins despite three generations in France; the turfspeak Franglais: le lad, le boxe, le canter, le crack jockey, le outsider and so on. It all added up to a pulsating racing industry in which the odour of newly minted franc notes was as rich and persuasive as the smell of new-mown hay.

Were he an anxious man, the transplanted Breasley might have reflected broodingly on his rather barren first training season; the furtive noise and movements of iconoclasts eagerly gouging at a living legend's feet quarrying for traces of clay. Mouths holding fat cigars or wisps of hay had bandied about the apocryphal rumour that his take-off came only after the incomparable Australian trainer, Tommy Smith, on an English visit, had set him to rights.

Breasley had scoffed at all of this: 'Of course there were problems when I started training. It was difficult to get things and staff the way I wanted them and I myself probably wasn't fully prepared'. Effort wasn't lacking; in

Scobie Breasley becomes Champion jockey riding Dario at Lingfield in 1969.

Breasley wins the King George and Queen Elizabeth stakes on Ballymoss in 1958 three lengths ahead of the Queen's Almeira.

156

his first five months Scobie shed weight from his normal, sparse 112 pounds. The truth was Scobie had not anticipated stepping in his fifties onto the tricky slats of the training treadmill. While his 3,000 winners over forty years had massaged ambition and bank balance he owed the sport nothing; he had paid a huge price in effort and injury.

'I had thought that at the end of it I would try to get into the bloodstock side. I have always kept interest back in Australia and I had marvellous contacts all over the world. But Mae kept saying I would not have enough to do, and I would be miserable playing golf all the time. I think she and Gordon (Sir Gordon Richards for whom he rode) rather pushed me into it. In the winter of 1968 I had told Gordon the next would probably be my last season and he said I ought to go and train. Then in the summer we heard the Bessie Nightingale was keen to sell South Hatch and before I could really say "no" it was mine'. South Hatch Stables, set above Epsom Town within a mile of Tattenham Corner, was where Mrs. Nightingale's husband Walter had trained for Sir Winston Churchill.

An apt connection: like Breasley, Sir Winston had made his most glowing achievements at a mature age. Scobie was already thirty-six, and being retired in some quarters, when he first came to England in 1959. In Australia, he had already been champion apprentice, three times champion jockey and won four Caulfield Cups; only the Melbourne Cup had eluded him. His wife Mae says he was talking of England and riding in the Derby even before they were married on November 5th, 1935 (the day Lester Piggott – whom he later pipped for two English championships – was born in Wantage). Scobie said: 'Although things were going well in Australia, in the autumn of 1949 my great friend and supporter Harry Ford was going to England and I asked him if he could fix me up with a job'.

Ford had no trouble. So the 1950 flat racing season began with English racegoers preparing to watch A. (for Arthur) Breasley as contract rider for cinema millionaire J. V. Rank's stable at Druids Lodge near Salisbury in Wiltshire (famous for early twentieth-century betting coups pulled by the Druids Lodge Confederacy). Sadly Ford died that summer and never realised how great a favour he had done his protégé.

After riding seventy-three winners in his first season, and sixty-six in his second (including the Two Thousand Guineas on Ki Ming), Breasley followed his original plan and went home. There he won another local championship and his fifth Caulfield Cup but an urgent telegram from trainer Noel Cannon brought him back to ride eighty-three winners in the 1953 flat season.

Then, in May 1954, came near tragedy: a race fall that brought brutal injuries. It was at the now-defunct London track below Alexandra Palace. Laid out in very limited space, the course was saucepan-shaped, with starting and finishing straights up and down the handle. The tricky camber at the edge of the saucepan was treacherous footing for horses. Many slipped and fell. One victim was the all-too-aptly named Sayonara with Scobie up. As Breasley fell, the back of his head hit one of the concrete uprights supporting the rails: his skull and spinal column at the neck were damaged.

Medical examination showed the base of the skull and spinal cord were in such shreds that if doctors had operated immediately, as they had planned, it would almost certainly have fatally severed the connections. Even after three weeks in hospital, Breasley was left partially paralysed and had no sense of balance. But any bookmakers who might have quoted odds of a million to one against his ever winning a championship overlooked the steely toughness behind the slow smile of the man from Wagga Wagga.

'Balance was the difficult thing' he says now. 'But I was very lucky to have surgeon Billy McKissick to treat me. He let me persevere and (Australian golfer) Norman von Nida and I used to go to the golf course every day and I would try to hit a ball around. Things gradually came back. Then, just before the Goodwood meeting in August, I got on a horse again and every-thing seemed all right.' At Chantilly, twenty-two years later, Scobie still felt some discomfort in his neck on a raw February morning; he always would.

'It was fine while I was riding. But Mae and some others close to me knew that for a long time I had to hang on to a horse for a second or two after I had dismounted, to get my balance back. I tried to take things easy; no late nights, not too many dawn gallops and everything picked up very well.'

Laconic. A typical Breasley understatement. The next season he rode his first century: 109 winners. Having signed for Sir Gordon Richards, he in-creased this to 143 in 1956, then 173 in 1957 for his first jockey championship, the first Australian jockey to do this since Frank Wooton in 1912. He was top man again in 1961-2-3, only once failing to ride one hundred winners a season until his final year in 1968; the exception, in 1966, was ninety-seven.

Arid statistics. With Breasley, the style, which became an integral part of the English racing year, was the thing. He used touch and judgment rather than brute force and in a finish would almost never strike with his whip; it was more a conductor's baton to stretch the animal to maximum effort. Sir Gordon Richards, himself twenty-five times champion jockey before turning trainer, enthused: 'He was a great, great rider. For a trainer the wonderful thing was that there has never been a gentler champion. When horses came back from a (Breasley) race they were happy in themselves; you could go straight on with their programme.'

Distant early days at Caulfield with renowned trainer Paddy Quinlan had paid off. 'I remember that if you were half a second out on the time you were supposed to work, he would kick you up the backside,' says Breasley. Thus he developed the uncanny judgement of pace he used with a magician's skill, adapting it to the immensely varying demands of the many courses around Britain. Erstwhile observers can still contentedly fill their mind's eye with the classic Breasley race, the horse picking up his field from far back with a steady rhythmical run, as if being wound on a string, to get in front on the line.

The non-aesthetic and voluble racegoers clutching sweat-streaked betting tickets didn't always appreciate Scobie's visible finesse whenever his penchant for the inside rail occasionally got him trapped, or whenever the gentle touch did not quite pull off the race. But in later years, more fascinating than his artistry were his nerve and toughness: Breasley in his forties, then fifties, lucky to be alive but still going the shortest way through a pack without a tremor and surviving six hundred rides a season with a smile.

Togetherness: Breasley on Big Deal in September 1967.

Breasley's secret was simple: 'looking after myself'. Perhaps in part to recuperate from that horrible Alexandra Park fall, he adopted a life-style more akin to a stockbroker than a success-hungry jockey. He wisely eschewed hectic dawn gallops, travelled everywhere by chauffeur-driven Rolls and wintered with Mae on the St. James's coast of Barbados in a holiday home named Lor'Zonkel (for daughter Loretta and grandchildren Zonda and Kelly). Scobie photographs breakfasting in bed with the newspapers; long relaxed hours on golf courses; languid habits that brought envious and sardonic remarks. But they added up to a routine that paid off. Riding at a natural 112 pounds, boosted by Mae's unfailing support and good humour, he was a man whose fitness absurdly belied his years. Nobody knew this better than arch-rival Piggott who learned of Scobie's brilliance the hard way and then said: 'He was a great, great champion and tremendously hard to beat.'

While his last five years of riding brought no championship, they did yield some of his finest moments. In 1964, as a fifty-year-old grandfather, and at the thirteenth attempt, he fulfilled his abiding ambition by winning the Derby on Santa Claus. The Irish-trained colt, a hot favourite, responded to typical Breasley aplomb, threading through the field and swooping in the last hundred yards to win by a length. Two years later Breasley won his second Derby, on Charlottown, by a neck, with another display of his sublime craft.

But those computer-exact calculations could not altogether offset his loss of bodily resilience; inevitable falls were now not shrugged off easily. In 1966 a back-shaking fall grounded him for two months. Although Scobie topped the century again in 1967 he decided on turning fifty-four that 1968 would be his last season. Training became his new life.

South Hatch Stables contained more than forty boxes but forty winners a season didn't come until the final year before he left for France. However, the pioneer and steadfast support of Lady Beaverbrook, widow of the newspaper magnate, and of octogenarian Angus Kennedy were rewarded with big winners, such as Lady Beaverbrook's 1972 success with Biskrah in the Doncaster Cup and Royben's 1971 Ayr Gold Cup victory for Angus Kennedy.

Then came the two most crucial elements in Scobie's training career; in 1972 he first linked with Tikkoo (Steel Pulse winning the Irish Derby) and, two years later, Wally Mills joined the stable. Wally, four years older than Scobie, had been head lad to the famous George Todd until Todd retired. His choosing to come to Chantilly with Breasley's team was one of the most encouraging aspects of the move.

'I wouldn't have come for anyone but the guv'nor,' said silver-haired Mills, surveying the straw-lined horse boxes that French champion jockey Yves St. Martin had described as 'the best turned-out in Chantilly'. Wally was sure the team would conquer. 'The guv'nor takes so much trouble and we have some really nice horses'.

Breasley wins the 1966
Derby in a photo-finish
against Pretendre and
Black Prince.

By the autumn of 1976 Scobie had proved himself a court card in Chantilly's pack in a way he had never done at Epsom. His horses had won more than 30 races including six Group 1 (top stakes races) and more than £350,000. His horses also won in Germany and England and this whole haul was without the bonus of a single major prize and without a champion horse. It was by far Scobie's best training year. Then, one of its sunniest days turned to thunder and the Chantilly connection was over.

At Longchamp on September 12th, the favourite, Java Rajah, gave the stable its second big Tierce success by winning the £10,000 Prix Omnium. Then the nastiness began. The racing authorities announced that illegal traces of caffein had been found in the post race urine test, the first positive result of its kind to be found under French flat racing rules for a quarter of a century. Java Rajah was automatically disqualified but Breasley and Tikkoo were seething. Tikkoo was particularly incensed that Scobie was not allowed to have an independent analysis of the offending sample and he stood firmly behind Breasley's statement that he had 'absolutely no idea how the caffein could have gotten into Java Rajah's system.'

There were whispers that the jingoistic French had taken vicious revenge, through Tikkoo for Trepan, the Chantilly horse whose positive dope test disqualified him from major victories at Ascot and Sandown earlier that summer. The French authorities tried to make peace with Tikkoo but because they would not budge from a rigid interpretation of the rules the tanker tycoon set about dismantling his new French empire, held a large dispersal sale, sent Scobie off to America with a select thirty-six and left the French battle to continue on through a suit against the French authorities at the International Court at The Hague.

Tikkoo's disillusionment appeared to go even deeper because, come the thaw in the spring of 1977, he announced that he no longer had anything to do with the horses that had seemed to be such a colourful part of his life. A month earlier the faithful Wally Mills was finally refused a work permit at Belmont and so the last remaining link with Scobie's Chantilly-beating team was sadly dissolved.

Once again Scobie seemed trapped on the rails. But then that has been his style. So calm in the storm that you could bet your last dollar that he will make the shore . . . even if it's by a neck in the last stride.

163

19 JOHN HUSTON, M.F.H.

Liz Harries

'Risk, not to say recklessness, are virtual reflexes in him'. Thus wrote a screenwriter, the late James Agee, shortly after meeting film director John Huston in 1950. Agee swiftly learned how eagerly and capriciously Huston injected risk into his moviemaking. The following year they collaborated on *The African Queen*, now the world's most recurring television programme. With gallows humour, Huston chose to film it in the malarial, debilitating heat of the Belgian Congo. It was the worst climate for drinking that two accomplished tipplers, Humphrey Bogart and Huston, ever had to endure. Though Huston later carted himself and muttering film units to a great many almost as insufferable.

Risk was an ingredient John Huston happily embraced during almost twenty years of riding to hounds with the famous County Galway Hunt – the Blazers. Foxhunting anywhere has ingrained physical perils; it's that kind of sport. But that part of County Galway which is the Blazers' hunting terrain is tougher and more dangerous than most. Fields are small and totally surrounded. Riders have to jump fifty or sixty stone walls on an average day's hunt. Many of the fields have no gates at all; to get out a rider has to jump his perhaps tired horse or dismantle the wall.

Often a huntsman, taking his horse over an apparently simple three-foot-high wall, discovers in mid air that the drop back to earth on the far side is six or seven feet. Or he suddenly spots, too late, a flock of sheep or redundant farm machinery tucked under the lee of the wall. (Huston used this hazard to give his murderous villain his grisly come-uppance at the end of that wry practical joke of a film, *The List of Adrian Messenger*, part of which he filmed in this area. The killer, played by Kirk Douglas, had hidden a massive roller, bristling with cruel spikes, against a fence, hoping a fox-hunting heir he wanted to expunge would impale himself on them. Instead, Douglas ended up skewered onto the roller). A famous show jumper,

Participating in the film *Marquis de Sade* only as an actor, John Huston was content to allow his handsome white steed to hog the camera.

165

Tommy Brennan, was said to have jumped a fierce (huge) wall, and dropped seven or eight feet on the far side. On landing, he was horrified to note he and his mount had soared over a thatched cottage hard against the fence and a woman had just opened the front door and walked outside, only feet from where they came down. For a time in Galway there was also the danger of finding yourself the landing ground for a notorious and reckless local priest, once banished by his Bishop for overindulgence in hunting.

Experienced Blazers members, Galway-bred and always in good riding fettle, could cope with all of this. But when Huston, a hunting novice, joined the club in 1960, he had no introductory phase: he simply clambered onto a horse and set off. In his years of active riding there he often flew back from filming physically unfit and not having been on a horse for months. Yet he loved the sport so much he was back in the saddle straight away. Astonishingly he would finish his first hunt after absence in fine shape, seldom having taken a tumble; this said a great deal for his instinctive horsemanship. His dash and adhesion to his horse's back certainly impressed Gil Morrisey, for many years the Blazers' terrier man (in charge of the Jack Russells and of digging out a fox gone to earth). 'Mister Huston didn't fall often, only when he was tired. He would just dust himself off and be on his way again', he said.

In truth, John Huston was a far-from-classic seat for riding to hounds. He was said to have learned to ride during a two-year stint in the Mexican cavalry, from which he emerged at twenty-one as a lieutenant. By European standards he rode long-stirruped, with the rolling, casual style more that of a Rio Grande vaquero than a hunting gentleman. Mounted, he had the poise and easy confidence of a cattle baron, such as his father, Walter Huston, a magnificent actor, played in his last film, *The Furies*.

He needed those low-slung stirrups to accommodate his six-foot-four-inch height comfortably. He also needed a sturdy mount to carry his two hundred pounds without wilting.

He had one in Frisco, his favourite hunter, who stood sixteen hands and was a horse of striking intelligence and beauty. Because Huston rode on a loose rein, Frisco and his other mounts needed the additional qualities of not taking hold (running away) or tending to stop at those fearsome walls. Lord Hemphill, of Tullira Castle, near Galway City and one of his Associate Joint Masters, described Huston's hunting talents as 'functional'. But he added: 'He was a very brave man, seemingly devoid of the sense of fear and rode courageously over high walls and rocky terrain'.

When the Joint Committee invited him, in 1960, to become Joint Master of the Blazers, he had no illusions about why the honour had been directed at him. The answer was simple: money. The hunt needed his financial support, and he willingly gave it. He cherished the chase, and Ireland itself, too much to fret about keen motives. He wisely knew his limitations as a foxhunter. Once he became M.F.H. he contentedly sank back into the ranks of the followers. He never hunted hounds himself or acted as field master (the member who takes charge of the followers, making sure they don't ride over hounds or inflict unnecessary damage to farmers' land, and other foolishnesses). He never asked his horse to attempt too much, was unfailingly courteous to fellow followers (in a manner befitting an American southerner – he was born in Missouri, the grandson of a professional gambler) and was adept at catching loose horses and reviving the fallen.

It took much brio for an American-born immigrant (Huston reversed the historical tide by settling in Ireland and becoming a naturalised citizen) to slot so comfortably into one of the world's renowned hunts. Especially in Galway, where the baying of trained fox hounds has been as common as birdsong for almost two hundred years.

In the late eighteenth century a member of the Persse family of Moyode (early on they were almost the spinal column of the County Galway Hunt) hunted a fine pack, fine because he paid top prices to get the best. While Mr Persse himself modestly wore the traditional scarlet jacket, he tricked out his hunt servants in plush orange livery and mounted them on fine steeds. In 1803, he split the pack, giving most to his nephew Robert Parsons Persse, who controlled the Castleboy Hunt. Those he kept for his son were handed down to his grandson, Mr Burton R. P. Persse, in 1848. Burton Persse, the first, considered by all as one of the best huntsmen of his day, led his hunt for a record thirty-three years. Legend has it that the 'Blazers' gained their name one boisterous evening when Persse's hunt and another, the Ormond, were whooping it up at an inn at Burr village. By accident, or perhaps to cap the evening, the inn burned to the ground. Hence the Blazers.

Similar high spirits apparently earned Mastership of the hunt for John Dennis, a clergyman's son, after the elder Burton Persse's death created the vacancy. Dennis challenged Barry Bingham, a brother of Lord Clanmorris, to a race over a course of twenty-five walls. Dennis was to ride his chestnut mare, who had already covered twenty miles that day, without saddle, bridle, spur or whip (his riding crop was a cabbage stalk). He won. This lively fellow was also reputed to have won a four-mile steeplechase on a blind horse at Roscommon (a course on which he later crashed so badly his injuries forced him to resign his post). A veteran hunt member of his day said of Dennis: 'He is the most brilliant rider and the most perfect master of equitation I ever came across, the finest steeplechaser in England or Ireland, the quickest and most daring rider to hounds'.

This fearless exuberance has always been part of John Huston's character and may help in part to explain his talent to get along with the Irish. This is no mean achievement among a people who believe simplistically that Americans are just two things – wealthy and gullible. Huston is also a man of great charm and persuasive powers. He has proved this through cajoling the late L. B. Mayer, a towering philistine, into backing his obviously non-commercial film *The Red Badge of Courage*. And even more, through somehow enticing pampered, demanding actors and film crews to brave baking heat, reptiles and cafard on hellhole locations. He took, as mentioned earlier, Bogart and Kate Hepburn to the Congo for *The African Queen*; Errol Flynn and Trevor Howard to Equatorial Africa (daytime temperatures 124°F) for *The Roots of Heaven*; Clark Gable and Marilyn Monroe to salt flats in Nevada for *The Misfits*; Richard Burton and Ava Gardner to Puerta Vallerta in Mexico for *The Night of the Iguana*. In each place, Huston was the only person impervious to heat, disease, mosquitoes, bad liquor and boredom. At the end of a frazzling day's shooting, he would be as unruffled and crisply attired as if he had just stepped out of the barber's shop at the Beverley Hilton in Hollywood. Maddening to the afflicted, yet nobody ever pulled a gun or knife on Huston; he could soothe with a soft word and wide grin. His spruceness was evident whenever the Blazers gathered. His pink jacket, silk top hat, snowy white stock around his neck, were always the most immaculate in sight; you could see the gloss of his beautifully cut riding boots three fields away.

John Huston used his love of hunting and the tough Galway terrain when shooting the climactic sequence of his quirky thriller *The List of Adrian Messenger*.

It was soon after finishing *Red Badge* in 1952 that John Huston first came to Ireland, renting a glorious house, Courtown, in County Kildare. Though he had not hunted before, he soon realised that foxhunting was his sport. With natural aptitude, he hunted in counties Limerick, Meath, Kilkenny, Tipperary and Kildare. On a hunting trip to Craughwell in Galway, he saw St Clerans, a somewhat run-down Georgian mansion of cut limestone against the setting sun and knew he must have it. Set in a hundred acres, the six-bedroomed big house had all the trappings to make him a country squire: a smaller second house, stable yards, stable yard flats, groom's house, miniature lake, trout stream. He poured in tens of thousands of dollars installing air-conditioning, a sunken Japanese bath in the basement, a four-poster Renaissance bed, the finest collection of pre-Colombian art in Europe (an interest developed through friendship with a South American jockey in the States) and converted part of the stables into an artist's studio to paint in (and pretty fairly, too). He restored the stables to suit the comfort of the Thoroughbred horses that arrived later; he had built superb hunters' loose boxes with oak doors and cast iron railings.

Huston had an eye and instinct for good horses. When he had time he loved to drive around the lanes of Galway, hoping to discover another top class horse or pony by the shape of its ears over a wall or its silhouette on a hill. Aided by his tireless secretary, Miss Beatrice O'Kelly, he built up a grand herd of Connemara ponies, selecting at random from yards and fields. He exhibited them widely, achieving the ultimate for the breed – winners' ribbons at the Connemara Show at Clifton.

The hounds are readied for director Huston's instructions to begin the next take in *The List of Adrian Messenger* in which the victim was not the fox but the mass murderer.

He dispersed the herd in 1962 to make way for Thoroughbred stock Some mares that Lady Hempbill, at Tulira Castle, bought from him helped form the basis for her world-famous Connemara Stud, which exports the ponies all over the world. When buying or selling broodmares and their youngstock, he seldom needed professional advice; he had the needed sixth sense.

While horses were his main interest, John Huston sometimes followed a proper squire's two other main interests – fishing and shooting. His fishing, however, was so wild and undisciplined that his prize catch one windy day was Beatrice's earlobe. Shooting he indulged with typical Hustonian verve. The sight of a couple of lads coming late at night with a few brace of duck or snipe into one of the oysters and Guinness bars he frequented would trigger off an immediate hunting party. Cadging a couple of pennies he would telephone St Clerans for the guns and dogs to be brought around without delay. Those he could beguile into the night party (and few could resist him) bundled into cars and vans and roared away into the night. So visiting American female friends would find themselves in high heels, Givenchy dresses or Bonwit and Teller suede suits, blundering through the darkness into brambles or leaping fences (Huston: 'You'll be okay, honey') to sink thigh deep into bogs. Again the Huston grin would calm them and the St Clerans staff would be up all night restoring damaged garments.

But, like anything else, it had to end. In 1970, Huston retired as M.F.H. of the Blazers after ten years. The Hunt presented him with a memento, a silver trophy of a fox that he thinks more of than his several Academy Awards for both screenwriting and direction. While a veteran director, he was still much in demand. Ireland became impractical; he was too often away filming on location to afford the enormous expense of St Clerans. It went on the market. He replaced it with a single-storey crofter's cottage in Lettermullen, on the furthermost island of three on the north of Galway Bay (in five years he did not manage to get back to stay there for a single night). In 1974, bowing to work and the dislike his new wife, Shane, had for the Irish, he sold his bloodstock, hung up his riding boots and returned to California. He would turn seventy in 1976; long return visits to his adopted land of Ireland were possible rather than probable.

A Blazers hunt seemed the less without the big, stylish man with the booming laugh and exquisite manners; the unselfish reviver of the fallen. No disciple of caste and privilege, he might just have been the most democratic M.F.H. the sport has known.

20 JAMES CAAN'S PRIVATE OBSESSION – THE RODEO

John Sheppard

Elsewhere in this book Dotson Rader shows us the lot of American rodeo performers. It's no gravy train. Most cowboys, in the old tradition of the West, remain dirt-poor. The system – plunking down twenty-five or fifty dollars to risk your hide against winning a few hundred (or most likely nothing) – keeps them that way.

Any rodeo cowboy with a fat wad of dollars in his Levis must have earned it doing something else. There has been one such well-heeled competitor moving in and out of the circuit since the early 1970s. Name of James Caan, a movie actor. Mr Caan, star of Rollerball, Funny Lady *and other successful films, shells out a lot of money, and suffers a lot of pain, pursuing this foolhardy recreation. So, the pertinent question must be: why does he do it . . . ?*

We fade in with a medium shot of James Caan in the living room of his house on Sunset Strip in Los Angeles. Clad in Caan formal (T-shirt and well-worn jeans), he is bellowing business over the phone to his agent a few miles away in Beverly Hills. He could communicate just as well if he dispensed with Mr Bell's mischievous device; his decibel power is impressive. As he talks, Caan paces his lean, hard-muscled frame back and forth. Now and then his left hand cleaves the air. If his voice is loud it has the right emphatic tone of a man who is turning down an offer to star in a movie for two million dollars and ten per cent of the gross.

'Nah, nah, nah. I don't want . . . Look, it's my decision and I'm saying shove it'.

In matters of finance Caan would seem to be a very fussy man. Well, what sum of money would make his eyes light up? That's easily answered: one hundred and twenty-five dollars. Disciples of clean, pure logic would aver that Mr Caan had stripped his gears, shortcircuited behind the forehead. Not a bit of it. He simply likes to keep money in perspective. That two million and ancillary lettuce was a producer's offer for him to appear in a western film. But, after scanning three or four pages of the script he had decided it was a crock of . . . er . . . garbage. Besides, he couldn't endure even the thought of spending two months on location with some of the people slated to appear in the movie with him. As for the $125, Caan did in fact earn that very amount for one afternoon's work – tough and dangerous work.

He says it was the most satisfying pay cheque he ever received: the prize money for winning his first roping competition at a rodeo. He has since won several more. Each time the small boy's spirit that has a ninety-nine-year lease inside him has whooped with delight. 'Those wins made me prouder than my Oscar nomination for *The Godfather*', he admits.

This confession doesn't betray a cavalier, off-hand attitude towards his trade; Caan is a serious and enterprising actor. What it does spell out is his fierce pleasure in courting broken bones and mashed insides riding and roping on sunbaked arenas throughout the United States.

He suffers for it, having endured countless bruises and rope burns in crashing falls from broncos and steer roping efforts that have gone wrong. Caan is lucky still to have a thumb attached to his right hand. In 1974 he took part in a rodeo 'jackpot' tournament in which a big field of cowboys ante up a few dollars each to compete in several events. He came to grief as one of a two-man team roping fully-grown, 750-pound steers. Galloping at full tilt, he lassooed his animal and spun two fast loops to secure the lariat to the saddle horn. One loop trapped his thumb and almost ripped it off. While the tendons were massively ripped, Caan thought he had got off lightly: 'Why, I've seen thumbs break off and fly forty feet in the air,' he grinned. The thumb was out of action for eight months, forcing him 'to stir my coffee with a spoon for a change'.

Some months after the accident, the thumb was still noticeably bandaged when he was presented to Queen Elizabeth at the Royal Premiere of his film *Funny Girl* in London. The Queen, well versed in the hazards of riding horses, was most solicitous. Caan's mother, Sophie, often gazes adoringly at a photograph of that encounter, which shows the Queen's gloved hand seeking a careful route past James's maimed digit for the Royal handshake.

A mother can admire a son's dash and stoicism. Others who orbit around the movie superstar that Caan has become are less ecstatic. In Los Angeles an active sub-industry has sprung up of attorneys who block out watertight clauses that bar Caan from rodeo work between signing a film contract and his finishing his work on that movie. 'It's in my contract that I can't even *think* about rodeo during a picture,' Caan sighs. His agents and promoters are very moist-palmed about the whole business; they reason that an actor who can be offered two million dollars plus for a single film should confine himself in his more audacious moments to a heavy game of backgammon.

Caan on horseback with rope in hand competes in one of the toughest of sports, but it is tranquil compared to the blood-drenched mayhem of Rollerball, the allegorical sport of one of his most successful films.

Mr Paul Bloch, senior vice-president of Rogers & Cowan, Caan's public relations consultants, was very cagey about his client's ride-'em-cowboy behaviour. When I wrote to him for information, Mr Bloch replied: 'There really is no written material on Mr Caan and his rodeo experiences. There's been little press on these activities because Mr Caan has chosen to keep a low profile in this area.' Perhaps the jarring thought of Caan's persistently low profile in the arena – sprawling flat on his back in the dust – encouraged Mr Bloch to deflect the inquiry.

All this forehead mopping and *angst* does not bother Caan in the slightest. One of the strongest characteristics he shares with all rodeo performers is a savage sense of independence. The instant he wraps up his own chores on any picture, he leaps into his fanciest auto, a pickup (utility) truck, and roars off to a rodeo somewhere.

'When I'm not working, they can't tell me what to do,' he says. 'Still, I don't blame 'em for working up a head of steam about it'.

Caan admits that the pain and maddening inconvenience of that busted thumb did give him pause about the chances of getting crippled in the rodeo arena. He makes immense sums of money as an above-the-title actor but needs it all; he supports up to twenty people, including his retired parents.

However, he gave the grisly prospects programme only one quick run through his mental projector before pulling it out. He contends, or rationalizes, that his rodeo work is both vital therapy and an effective purgative that flush the bile, poisonous gases and sediment of Hollywood's worst aspects from his system.

'Don't get me wrong: I love working in motion pictures. But once in a while you've got to clean it out of you. That's what roping does for me.' Caan has a true, peculiarly-American, passion for the dirt of the arena. 'It's clean and the whole thing is simple, basic, honest, wholesome, rough and tough. Besides, I just love playing the part of a cowboy. But it's not all acting. When you're taking on a mean animal in the ring, you can't fake it; it's the real thing. You leave the phony stuff far behind you, back in L.A.'

Caan is an obsessive and ferocious competitor; a friend says: 'When Jimmy loses at anything, he's as much fun as a carbuncle'. Yet he is surprisingly humble about his roping skills. 'I'm not bad but I'd have to get out the begging bowl if I tried to make a living from it against professionals who've been roping thirty steers a day for ten or twenty years. These fellers really love their way of life. And why not? It's clean and they've got no attachments, no responsibilities, no bills pouring in.

'And they haven't got much money pouring in either. Put up fifty bucks busting your ass to win maybe a hundred, and pay all your medical bills on top of that. They are wonderful people and very, very tough; you'll find no-one anywhere who is tougher than a rodeo cowboy.'

Caan's speciality at rodeos is calf-roping. Fiercely aggressive, the actor strives to advance his so-far moderate skills towards those of such as Californian Derrill Hester, here making something difficult look pretty easy.

Caan knows the gruelling economics of his strange pastime. In his first six or seven years in the rodeo rings, he won no more than $500 in prize money. In that time his expenses (travelling hundreds of miles to shows in Nevada, Arizona, Oklahoma, accommodation and so on) totted up to $15,000–$20,000.

How did this member of a middle-class Jewish family from the wide, open spaces of the Bronx in New York, ever get involved in these Tom Mix antics? In the early 1970s he was in Nebraska, making an excellent but now-forgotten film called *The Rain People*. On a day off, he went to watch cattle branding at a nearby ranch. He also said 'yes' when asked if he would like to help out; Caan's virility factor is high; he is permanently the Women's Lib's male chauvinist pig award winner. So he wrestled calves in ninety-five degree heat until sunset, then came back the next day to try his hand at roping. He hadn't told the cowboys he was an actor; they had accepted him as a lively visitor with plenty of zest and stamina.

His roping obsession made him a real pest. He bought a pair of roping horns mounted on a sawhorse and practised indoors, roping chairbacks, standard lamps, hatstands, bedposts and, very often, the blonde girlfriend then living with him.

As an ex-dancehall bouncer (from his starvation days as a young actor), Caan can look after himself. But through prudence – and genuine respect – he is never the movie star among cowboys; always just one of the rowdy, beer-swilling company. For one thing he is very proud to have been accepted into a tight fraternity (he belongs to the Rodeo Cowboys' Association). He feels very warmly about their comradeship. For another thing, uppity ways would make him an outsider among men he admires and who would be 'very dangerous to mess with'. 'But they know I'm there because I love roping and that I'll take my lumps along with the rest of them'.

Caan's hobby has been a blessing for the gauze and linament industries (and Alka-Seltzer as well, considering the dyspepsia he has wrought along Wilshire Boulevard). If admirers of his acting craft ever told him he had become half as good as Spencer Tracy, that would be the second finest compliment he could receive. The best? If he should some day accomplish a particularly skilful piece of roping and a fellow rodeo man tells him: 'Yep, a really pretty bit of ropin' there, Jimmy. Had a touch of McGonigal about it.'

Clay McGonigal, a stalwart of the 1890s and early 1900s, was *the* all-time legend among ropers in America's southwest. The record of twenty seconds he set in Tucson, Arizona in 1901 for roping and tying a steer in primitive conditions stood for almost twenty years – until McGonigal himself cut it by 1.25 seconds in Chicago.

To be compared to McGonigal, Caan would give . . . any advance on two million dollars and ten per cent of the gross?

21 RELUCTANT PARTNERSHIP
Norman Thelwell and his ponies

John Sheppard

Norman Thelwell doesn't care much for horses. Or ponies. He regards them, like sheep, cattle and poultry, merely as part of the country background. No need to get excited over them, he says.

Mr Thelwell's antipathy is his adult legacy of a childhood spent romping through the bleak, grassless streets of Birkenhead on Merseyside. To his urban child's eye a horse was a weary, plodding animal between the shafts of a baker's or coalman's cart. The strongest emotion Mr Thelwell can raise about equine creatures of any size or breed is one of the most basic in human nature: fear. The thought of moving within kicking or biting distance of even the most docile Shetland pony petrifies him. Now and then a character representing the Thelwell outlook will crop up in one of his renowned pony cartoons: a cowering, whitelipped figure backed into the far corner of a stall by a cantankerous pony or hiding crouched behind a haystack.

This anguish is a splendid counterpoint that enriches the gentle, uncomplicated and very English humour of his cartoons. It stands in such contrast to the dauntlessness, the absolute fortitude of the stubby-legged, button-nosed tots who ride that unique creature, the Thelwell pony. While now distinctive, they did not emerge from any calculated blueprint; they just happened in the same haphazard way, he contends, that all his good fortune has come to him.

'To be perfectly honest, I never thought of projecting anything specific. I think of myself purely as a light entertainer and nothing else. But there were a couple of incidents which I realise in retrospect did influence me about ponies and children.

'In the early 1950s, when we lived in the Midlands, there were ponies in a neighbour's field and little girls, really minute girls, on the ponies. One in particular used to walk into the field dressed in her hard hat and riding gear like a little general. When she approached her pony it would start to kick out at her. When I first saw this I felt like leaping over the fence to rescue her, except that I was frightened of the pony anyway. But the child was completely unperturbed; she simply dodged the flying hooves until she worked around to the pony's head, where she would take charge, then lead the pony away as docile as a puppy. The fearless quality of these children really staggered me.

" REMEMBER WHAT I TOLD YOU GIRLS,
NEVER LET HIM SEE YOU'RE AFRAID. "

A pioneer effort: the first pony drawing among many to appear in *The Sunday Express*.

'Another time, looking out of my window, I saw two small girls, mounted, and obviously having a quarrel. They were lashing at each other with their whips like a pair of knights jousting on horseback. They handled their ponies beautifully, manoeuvring them around to the most effective position to get in another swipe. For somebody like me, a cartoonist and non-rider, it was a lovely situation'.

To the diminutive Mr Thelwell, these children were all he could never be. His quiet recognition of their courage must have burrowed into his subconscious to start fermenting his first pony cartoon. It was an oblique inspiration, really an off-shoot of the major theme to which he had staked his claim as a *Punch* cartoonist – English country life. By this time, circa 1953, he had been contributing for some three years to the venerable humorous magazine, though still vibrating with surprise that his first tremulously-submitted effort had been accepted at all. He had no good reason to be so diffident: no other *Punch* cartoonist was tapping such a rich vein as Thelwell or producing work rendered in such profuse and exquisite detail. That pony cartoon was to be strictly a one-off thing, you understand; get it out of the way and then re-focus the brain on subjects he knew and cared more about.

It duly appeared showing a girl and newly-shod pony in a cluttered smithy with the blacksmith inquiring sweetly: 'How do they feel, then?' The caption was mainstream Thelwell: humour as gentle as a snowflake brushing against

The first of Thelwell's pony drawings ever published. Only the pleased response from *Punch* readers made him do another on a similar theme. All other pony drawings spring from this source.

" 'ow do *they* feel then? "

a cheek. Draughtsmanship, however, was still at an apprentice stage, revealing his admiration for, and the inspiration of, fellow-*Punch* artists, Ronald Searle, Anton and Sprod. Yet Thelwell's ambition to think small rebounded on him. Serves him right. That single drawing was the first brick in what proved to be a pleasure dome in Xanadu; it set Norman Thelwell on his way to becoming an international industry.He started, and remains, a reluctant tycoon ('I don't want to die like a millionaire.'); fame and riches were to creep up from behind and sandbag him.

In village and dale, horsey folk stirred; the first cartoon charmed and delighted them. Could Mr Thelwell draw another? Well, why not?

'To this day I can't remember what that second pony cartoon was about. Then the editor of *Punch*, Malcolm Muggeridge, I think, asked if I could feature them in a double page spread. My first response was: "Look, I've done two and have milked the subject dry". But I applied myself and the double page spread appeared. It drew another big response from readers.

'Then Bernard Hollowood took over as editor of *Punch*. He said: "Everyone is calling you a pony cartoonist, which is mad. We don't want any more of that". So I drew very few and, in fact, have drawn very few for *Punch* for many years. But once they were established, they literally took over on their own. It was never planned. The Thelwell pony was no lovingly or carefully devised animal; it just evolved'.

It certainly did, into one of the most distinctive creatures of its era; perhaps only Charles Schulz's hedonistic beagle Snoopy, from his *Peanuts* comic strip, has made such an impact in all parts of the world where people have access to the printed page. The ponies began to canter, then to gallop, all the way to the bank, their barrel bodies heaving, stumpy legs pumping, thick, unkempt manes flying and tiny riders bouncing up and down. Mr Thelwell recalls that a large British insurance company hitched them firmly to the gravy train.

'Three gentlemen in bowler hats and with furled umbrellas came down to my place from London.

'They wanted ponies to illustrate a pamphlet on life assurance "from the cradle to the grave". I honestly couldn't see the connection but said if they would change their motto to "from the pushchair to the bathchair" I would give it a go. They agreed, and after the pamphlet appeared, I was caught up in a ponies craze which still hasn't abated. I couldn't analyse the reasons for it. But it really doesn't matter. They're popular and that's that. These ponies have been a vein of gold – and I just stumbled upon them. I always seem to achieve things this way'.

To understand the range of commercial interest and the enormous popularity of his ponies (which also charm Brazilians, Russians and all Europeans) we have to digest another long list. Here are some of the items on which they have appeared: calendars, drinking mugs, egg cups, prints, tea towels, serviette rings, kitchenware, tumblers, mirrors, coasters and place mats, playing cards, greetings and Christmas cards, tee-shirts, posters, Irish dish cloths, diaries, clipboard folios. You name it and one version of it has almost certainly been Thelwellized.

In three months a 224-piece jigsaw sold 250,000 copies and the picture was then turned into a greetings card; the shrewd follow-up was a 400-piece jigsaw. An American firm brought out a logical item: a Thelwell hoofpick for removing mud from horses' hooves. Some items do not meet his standards. He ordered off the market a toy pony he considered very sub-standard.

Inevitably pirates slithered into action. From New York emerged Thelwell Productions Inc., marketing such items as playing cards, trays, blotters, goblets and coasters, all showing reproductions of Thelwell pony cartoons.

More identification, this time with the drenched girl in the pond.

"DON'T JUST SIT THERE, DEAR - HURRY HOME
BEFORE HE CATCHES A CHILL."

Their small oversight was to neglect to get Mr Thelwell's permission for any of this. The company was so brazen(and some of the products so shoddy) that Mr Thelwell ordered his lawyers to suppress them. But other pirates continue to exploit him unhindered. One of the busiest is a Japanese firm making a wide range of goods; they comfortably sold, for example, 20,000 table mats in Australia. In the studio of his Hampshire home, Mr Thelwell keeps a small set of this pirate's teeshirts, whose ponies, viewed up close, reveal Oriental brushwork.

'People ask me why I don't crack down on the Japanese. But, what am I to do? Give up work and start chasing around the world to stamp on people who have pinched something? It's ridiculous, even if you could do it. Are you going to fine them, put them in prison, or what? I get well paid for what I do and I do what I want and I live where I want and don't have the time or desire to get in pursuit of pirates.'

Mr Thelwell suffers more than enough aggravation from a legitimate company that handles franchises for Thelwell products in the United States. 'Anything you do has to be done well and I want some control. The thing I have against merchandising all round is that I am not consulted about what is going out with my name on it. This American company simply will not tell me what it is doing.' So people in many countries who go to horse shows (which he does not) and browse through the commercial stalls, know better than Thelwell the variety of stuff engraved, stamped, etched and transferred with his creations.

Loss of income from pirates does not bother Mr Thelwell 'I am approached to do four or five times as much work as I could accomplish. More money simply means more work for my accountant and more silly requests from the tax people. In some ways I was better off making £8 a week as an art teacher in the 1940s.' He is full of an honest man's indignity at the moral sleaziness of piracy and the cheap kitschiness of too many items illegally bearing his name. He is a man of high standards and professional pride. 'If I'm doing something for a fiver or free for a charity, I always do the very best work I am capable of doing'.

Now, as from his early childhood, drawing pictures is a compulsion, his one narcotic other than Gold Flake pipe tobacco and toy cigars. Yet he really could toss his brushes and pens aside and spend all his time watching the water slide through the four miles of the river Test (perhaps the best dry-fly trout fishing in the world) that he leases for £2,500 a year. Mr Thelwell, who would rather paint or draw water – placid, raging or wind-foamed – than anything else, has built two sluices and a hump-backed stone bridge on the river where it edges the foot of his garden. He fishes, but for the river's companionship, not to haul trout from its waters.

'I've as much money as I need. We could, in fact, live quite comfortably on the royalties from my books. I'm surprised that they all keep on selling well; they are all still in print'.

To be sure, his books – on ponies, fishing, boats, country life, gardens, motoring, dogs, buying a home – have been another bonanza. His publishers, Eyre Methuen, brought out the champagne and canapes in Manchester in 1975 to celebrate selling the one millionth Thelwell paperback. They weren't taking into account the hundreds of thousands of hardcovers sold. This enviable flow of royalties could be much higher because his American publishers, for reasons that baffle Mr Thelwell, have never brought him out in paperback. All in all, lovely returns for the two months' work a book usually entails.

Yet, for all the delight and the well-researched exactness of his fishing, boats and other books, so wonderfully rendered, those ponies and fearless riders are permanently superimposed on his reputation. In people's minds, that distinctive daddy-long-legs signature with the knobbed lettering means ponies quaint, cute, unusual, loveable and unlike any others. He has cornered the market, which is another irony to puff his pipe over.

'I do to some extent travel under false colours. I doubt that one eighth of my output is concerned with ponies; I'm forever turning down offers to do more. But people who do know something about horses somehow cling to the idea that I am an expert on them; that I must be able to handle them like Lester Piggott or Harvey Smith. I have even been asked to write on horses for *Encyclopedia Britannica*. These people think I am being coy, and a joker, when I say that I not only know nothing about them, but that I am scared stiff of them'.

Inevitably his mail contains a steady stream of invitations to judge at pony shows, to address equine folk of various persuasions. He declines almost all of them through basic honesty and because social gatherings of any kind scare him more than the horses themselves. Apart from attacking his nerves, these shindigs too often bring a brief social exchange he can do without: 'This is Mr Norman Thelwell'. 'Ah, yes, the pony man'. He doesn't nurse the irritation. 'You can't blame people for saying this because that is the way they came to know about you. It is natural for them to use a label to identify with another person, especially one who is well known'.

Norman Thelwell is a patient as well as a tolerant man. He needs patience to sift through the many suggestions he receives for cartoon ideas, from many countries, as well as Britain. The sifting chore also needs optimism: in more than twenty-five years as a known cartoonist, he has received just one suggestion he could use, out of hundreds.

'A farmer wrote to me with a simple idea. I knew immediately it was right because he had been thinking in terms of my work. That was the key. He suggested a small farmer sitting on a very large, a Thelwell-type tractor that was hauling a grasscutting harvester with a big waggon behind that for the mown grass. All big machines are very complicated the way I draw them and the farmer was singing: "One man went to mow . . .". I thought it was lovely and sent him off a fiver straight away. He was stunned and said he would give me plenty more suggestions, but he never had another one; it was a flash in the pan'.

Not surprisingly, children are among his most eager correspondents, with many offering suggestions. He is intrigued that as many American as British children write to him, though a large number of American letters are complaints about their trouble in getting hold of his books.

'American kids are totally precocious, very self-confident and so different from British children. They cheer me up with words of encouragement. One little American girl once wrote to me: "I am eight-years-old and know you will have a good career. Keep it up and some day you may be as famous as Charles Schulz" (the *Peanuts* creator). American adults are not as endearing. They send me pages of typed gags, all of them useless. America must be teeming with gagmen. Some of them must have been semi-professional but really, from the standard of their stuff, most of them must have starved to death by now'.

There was never any danger that Norman Thelwell would waste away in a cold-water garret. From his earliest years in Birkenhead ('I can never remember a time when I didn't draw') people could see he had talent. But he wasn't encouraged to exploit it; in a rough industrial city, drawing was considered as cissified as ballet dancing. His first job was a a junior clerk in an office for twelve and sixpence a week. In 1941 his call-up into the army at eighteen pushed him towards a life of cartooning. On service up country in India, he answered a bulletin board notice for people with magazine experience by plopping a sketchbook crammed with drawings of army life onto an officer's desk; his bid stemmed not from confidence but a desire to escape the drudgery of an infantryman's existence. A fast flip through, a nod and he was sent to Delhi as art editor of an Army magazine. 'I learned a great deal but still knew nothing about art. I decided that, after the war, I would tackle it from the beginning to find out if I had anything in common with people recognised as artists'.

So on demob he did that, enrolling at Liverpool College and cruising blissfully through a five-year degree in three. While still a student, he began freelancing, sending off work to little magazines such as the now-defunct *London Opinion* and *Lilliput*. He kept this up after graduation when he took a job teaching illustration at Wolverhampton College of Art. 'Sending off, say, three drawings a week for about four quid a time, I was earning much more than my basic salary of eight pounds a week. I can't claim to have ever had any trouble in selling my work', he says.

Yet . . . modest success could not easily persuade him to assault what he considered the citadel: *Punch* magazine. After much cogitating, he sidled up to them in 1950 by presenting some pocket cartoons, then very popular. Of course, they were accepted. A fellow teacher at Wolverhampton sniffed at these tiny efforts. 'Why don't you give them some detailed work; nobody really draws these days'. So Thelwell spent an entire weekend working up a single cartoon: a gypsy encampment of ornately-decorated caravans, elaborate costumes, mountains of intricate junk, with a passer-by commenting: 'It's their simplicity I envy'. Masses of beautiful detail; gentle yet vivid humour; the Thelwell cartoon had been born; you could almost smell the aroma of roast beef floating off the page. With much hard work but little effort he was to develop into the artist lauded as the most *English* of cartoonists. One year Lord Montagu used a Thelwell *Punch* cover on his Christmas card.

Mr Thelwell accepts the casting, if not his place on the list. It anchors him to England where he can keep on absorbing through mind and pores the drift of autumn smoke, the quality of soft light, the elms and poplars, the

Cool and daring, Norman Thelwell moves very close to a Shetland pony to autograph a copy of a book for a Thelwell-horsewoman come to life.

sheen on lake, river and fenwater, the geometry of hedgerows, wind-ruffled bird plumage, fishermen's garb and postures, the nautical madness that is weekend sailing. And small heroines with riding crops. Despite Inland Revenue bludgeoning, he would never flee from these delights, these vital sources; he regards all tax-exiles as 'traitors somehow'. His home at Herons Mead, Timsbury, in Hampshire, looks the perfect capital for Thelwell country: a much-converted vicarage residence of white chalk blocks set in seven acres; nearby a large, well-lit studio through whose windows he can see the River Test rippling by at the foot of sloped lawns; drone of bees and flap of birds' wings. The only un-English sight is his Volkswagen Combi van in the garage/stable.

Those studio windows throw regular yellow bars across the lawn as nightbird Thelwell ('I'm useless in the mornings') smokes and thinks, seeking the impregnation of fresh ideas. He has the usual problem: some surface easily, some emerge like teeth yanked with pliers.

'It seems to me the greatest things on earth are ideas – they are marvellous and beautiful or whatever. But, after a quarter of a century I still haven't worked out a formula or pattern for getting them to come through. I don't think there is any. Tomorrow could be barren, or fertile; I can't predict. Getting ideas is like twisting a radio dial until you tune in on something. I don't know when it is going to happen but I can recognise the feeling that something is about to. There is knowledge or some kind of sense working away in there somewhere.

'I don't try to analyse it; you only analyse when you have stopped doing something. To catch an idea on the wing you somehow have to try to keep on a mental plane that is free of too many entanglements. Once you get a subject you at least have some wood to start carving. You can break the idea down into its component parts to see what it's made of. This is the way I go about doing an entire book on a single subject, such as houses or boats. It has all been very hard work but I have been lucky because what comes out of this mysterious process has always been very saleable. A lot of people kill themselves in their effort to create and nobody wants to buy or even look at what they have done. Luck is there but to a great degree you create your own good luck through effort. And whether your work will survive is point-less; you'll be dead anyway. I don't kid myself that I'm a great painter. But I could earn my living from painting alone, admittedly at a lower level than I now enjoy. But I could have sold half that Winchester exhibition the day it opened. I do the sort of paintings people want to buy; that they feel they can live with. Do you really have to strive for more?'

'Drawing, for me, is a compulsive way of communicating. Has been all my life. I have always hated the business side of it. I find it distracting me from my main job. As you become more successful you get less time to do the work you want to do, which is, when you consider it candidly, more than a little stupid'.

Mr Thelwell wears success as neatly and unassumingly as the crisp sports shirt and immaculate slacks that are his version of the artist's smock. 'I do feel bemused about it all. It is all unbelievable. I never wanted to be a cartoonist for a start; that was all an accident. The height of my ambition was that I would never have to do a boring job like most people have to do'.

The man who started out with no ambition has no problem deciding how he'll spend his remaining time. 'I just want to draw. And if somebody wants to pay me for it, that is great. Just drawing. What else is there?'